新安縣志

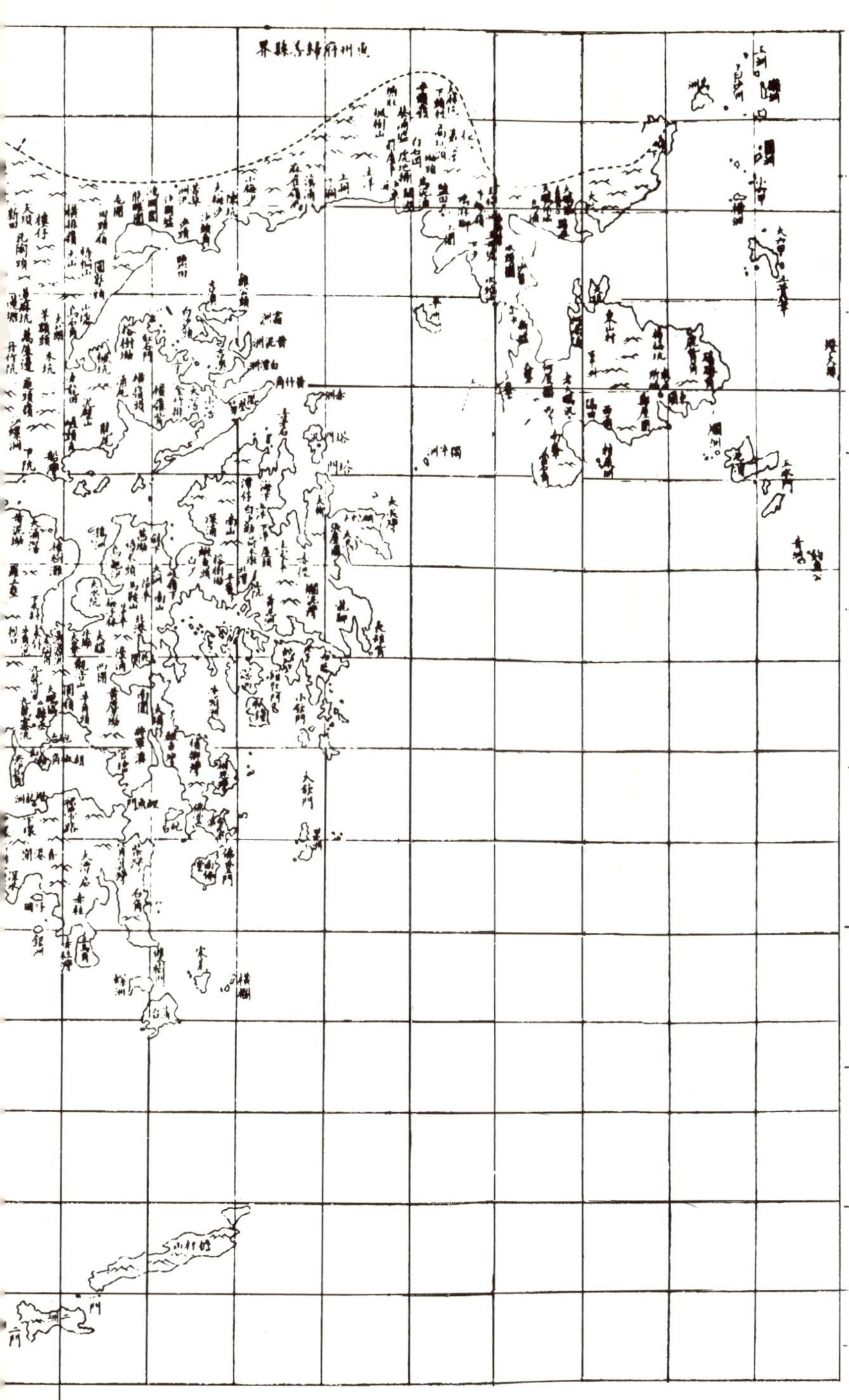

'Xin'an Xian Tu' (Map of Xinan County)
from Guangdong Yudi Quantu *(Maps of Guangdong),*
compiled by Zhang Renjun in 1897 and printed by Shijing Tang, Guangzhou.
A collection of maps of all the counties in Guangdong at that time,
with information on their history, boundaries, waterways, towns and
cities and officials, in Chinese.

NEW PEACE COUNTY

NEW PEACE COUNTY

A Chinese Gazetteer of the Hong Kong Region

by

Peter Y.L. Ng

prepared for press and with additional material by

Hugh D.R. Baker

HONG KONG UNIVERSITY PRESS

1983

ISBN 962-209-043-5

Printed by Liang Yu Printing Factory Ltd.
Yip Shing Industrial Building
9-11 Sai Wan Ho Street
Shau Kei Wan Hong Kong

To my mother Tong Lai Heung 湯荔香 (1904—1975)
in everlasting gratitude for her selfless devotion
to her family

CONTENTS

PREFACE

This book is adapted from the thesis, entitled *The 1819 Edition of the Hsin-an Hsien-chih: A Critical Examination with Translation and Notes* (subtitled *Hong Kong, Kowloon and the New Territories, 1644-1842*), which I submitted to the University of Hong Kong for my M.A. degree in 1961. To my surprise and pleasure, a large number of scholars have consulted the thesis and referred to it in their writings, and successive publishers of the Hong Kong University Press beginning with Mr Henri Vetch have expressed interest in publishing it.

Why then have twenty years elapsed from its original writing to its present publication? The reason lies in my own assessment that in order for publication to be viable, further research and rewriting must be done. Personal circumstances, however, such as my decision to leave academic life, my residence in Canada from 1967 to 1979, and the demands of business life in North America, have prevented me from undertaking such a project.

The turning-point came when during a visit to London in 1979 I discussed my thesis with Dr Hugh Baker, who innocently agreed to lend his time and expertise to the task of revising and editing it for publication. The resulting exercise has proved even more extensive than we at first intended. Not only has Hugh carried out further research and updated the thesis in the light of the scholarship that has been published in the intervening years, but he has also reorganized the material and provided additional translation and commentary where coverage has been inadequate.

My great debt is therefore due to Hugh for his friendship and cheerful collaboration, without which my thesis would still sit on the shelves of the Hong Kong University Library unpublished. I am also indebted to the various publishers of the Hong Kong University Press for their enduring interest and unfailing support. I should record my gratitude to my professor, Brian Harrison, to the late Professor Lo Hsiang-lin, and to Mr G.W. Bonsall, then Deputy Librarian of the University of Hong Kong, for their assistance in my research, and to Mr T.C. Lai and Dr B. Mellor for their friendship and encouragement. I am also grateful to Mr Lau Shung of the *Neutral Post* for supplying a copy of the 1979 reprint of the 1819 edition of the *Xin'an xianzhi*, to Miss Pat Weaver for her thoughtful and skilful preparation of the typescripts, and to Dr K.P.K. Whitaker

(Lai Po-kan) for her assistance with translation problems. My wife Julia, my children Juliana, Luciana, Peter and Andy have all contributed in their own way to the evolution of this book, and should not go unmentioned.

Although publication has been delayed for two decades, from a certain angle the present timing is excellent. As we draw nearer to 1997 when the lease of New Kowloon and the New Territories comes to an end, the future of Hong Kong looms in importance as an issue for discussion, speculation, and world-wide attention. But in order to come to grips with the future, it is necessary to understand the past. This book is filled with examples of how events and conditions before 1842 have helped to shape and influence life in Hong Kong even to this day. Just as contemporary Hong Kong cannot escape from its pre-1842 history, Hong Kong after 1997 will not be able to escape from what has taken place before then, whether we like it or not, and historians are likely to agree that Hong Kong has assumed a burden of history grotesquely out of proportion to its small size and humble origin. It is hoped that this book will contribute to the understanding of Hong Kong's past and present as it develops its extraordinary destiny.

Kellett View, Hong Kong — *Peter Y.L. Ng*
November, 1981

INTRODUCTION

In 1841 the British Superintendent of Trade at Canton, Captain Charles Elliot, negotiated the cession of the island of Hong Kong as one of the terms of the Convention which was to end the Opium War between China and Britain. Lord Palmerston, the Foreign Secretary in London, greeted the news with disgust and the much-quoted description of the place as 'a barren island with hardly a house upon it'. The Convention was not signed and Elliot was recalled from his post, but the cession of Hong Kong was retained as one of the terms of the Treaty of Nanking which was ultimately ratified in 1843.[1]

It is hard to blame Palmerston for his opinion of Hong Kong: the Chinese government's opinion of it was probably little different from his, and they should have been in a much better position to judge its value. But to the Chinese Emperor in far off Beijing Hong Kong was an insignificant rock in an undesirable sea off the coast of a minor county on the fringes of his empire. The Chinese maps of the area did nothing to enhance Hong Kong's importance: indeed in the 1822 edition of the Guangdong provincial gazetteer the map of the county of Xin'an in which Hong Kong lay did not show the island at all.[2]

The most up-to-date version of the gazetteer of Xin'an County itself (the work which forms the subject of this book) was little better as a source of information. The maps in it had neither precision nor detail, and the island of Hong Kong did not appear as such on them. Nor was the text of much use, for the island merited no special mention, having no agriculture to speak of, no salt pans, no major settlements, and no strategic value in the all-important defence of the entrance to the Pearl River and the provincial capital, Guangzhou. The very way in which the administrative subdivisions of the county were arranged indicated how insignificant this part of its territory was felt to be: Map 8 shows the disproportionately large district in which Hong Kong fell and in which presumably it could receive but scant attention from the Assistant Magistrate in charge.

Without the accident of history which made an island base with a deep and sheltered harbour in the vicinity of Guangzhou a desirable acquisition for nineteenth century Britain the Hong Kong region would doubtless have remained in obscurity, and the writing of its history would have been as unnecessary and unlikely as the following quotation implies:

> Hong Kong itself finds no mention in Chinese histories nor has any ancient monument been found on it. The mainland territories have little more attention in Annals. Although not very far from Canton, the capital of Kwangtung Province of which they immemorially formed part, these areas were very much on the outskirts; they were what we should call 'bush', 'jungle' or 'bedu', in other countries, troublesome places where the inhabitants were bandits or pirates. In those days, governments, whether in Europe or China, found it unprofitable and usually unnecessary to poke their noses into such places.[3]

But Hong Kong's existence as an enclave of Western influence, as a meeting ground of two major cultures, and as a window on Chinese society has dramatically altered its importance as an area. Since 1841 it has not been possible to consign the region to administrative and historical oblivion, and with a concern for the recent past has grown interest in the pre-British past. For government officers wrestling with centuries-old land tenure problems, for historians anxious to trace out the influences which shaped the development of contemporary Hong Kong, for anthropologists scrutinizing traditional Chinese behaviours and organization patterns, for folklorists, linguists, archaeologists and many others the early history of the Hong Kong area offers itself as an important and rewarding study.

The 1819 gazetteer of Xin'an County constitutes the single large-scale, comprehensive work on the area before the coming of the British. Some of its limitations have already been mentioned, and it has to be said that it is not an outstanding example of its genre. It is amateurish, undetailed, sporadic in coverage in terms of time, space and topic, and, if Krone's account of 1859 is a fair test of its authenticity, frequently inaccurate. Yet it does provide a skeleton on which to build up the flesh of the historical picture, and it cannot but give some insights into the way of life and style of government of the region.

From Krone in 1859 through Sung in 1935-38, Balfour in 1940-41, Baker in 1968, to Hayes in 1977, many students of Hong Kong have turned to the gazetteer for assistance, and it is unlikely that its usefulness will fade with the passage of time. Herein lies the first justification for this book: it is hoped that by serving as a guide to the contents of the gazetteer it will provide some of the information required by future researchers as well perhaps as stimulating further research on the area.

The second justification is in introducing the composition and scope of a Chinese local gazetteer to those who have never been exposed to one. A glance at the 'Contents' of the 1819 edition is enough to show that this is more than just a history book. Natural history, geography, economy, anthropology, mythology, folklore, government, meteorology and much else is included, and categories which Westerners might keep separate intermingle here. Thus in the middle of a sequence of prosaic natural disasters can be found a comment linking plague with the appearance of blood in oysters,[4] and 'Ferries' is a subsection of the chapter headed 'Buildings'.[5]

Gazetteers were, in fact, a collection of facts and fantasies relevant to a particular area, be it province, prefecture, county, scenic mountain or whatever; but the 'relevance' depended very much on the views of those who compiled them, and this explains partly the great variation in quality and organization of these works. Probably the greatest influence on gazetteer writing was Zhang Xuecheng (Chang Hsüeh-ch'eng) 章學誠 :

> "The aim of the compiler of a local history," Chang maintained, "should not be to produce something pleasing to look at, but something actually useful; since times differ and situations change, old histories of a locality cannot include everything one may look for, and so there should be a new one compiled every thirty to one hundred years." Chang, it would seem, conceived a local history to be not merely a description or explanation of historical changes but a description of the present institutional and social situation viewed with a certain historical depth.[6]

Posterity has reason to be grateful to Zhang for his eclectic approach. A multipicity of disconnected detail is just as informative as a chronological account of events, and Zhang's method supplied both.

Gazetteers were written partly as local curiosities of interest to the small number of literate men living in the area covered. But by Ming and Qing times they had become increasingly important to officials serving, as they must, in provinces away from their native ones. For them a good local gazetteer was a vade-mecum which could serve as a guide to the alien ways of a new posting, and successive governments encouraged the writing of gazetteers accordingly. For later scholars these works have provided the data for studies of population, trade, food production, tax systems, market hierarchies, education, minority problems, social mobility, customs, government organization, irrigation techniques and a host of other matters.[7]

The third justification is, quite simply, that it has been an entertaining task to prepare this material and there is therefore hope that reading it will prove equally entertaining. The Xin'an gazetteer, unlike those for other parts of China, is constantly enlivened by reference to an area which is freely accessible and where survivals of what is recorded can be visited and compared: when the gazetteer speaks of the Beidu Monastery or the Amah Rock, both of which can still be seen in the New Territories, history suddenly comes alive. And more than one of the translated passages have been included for no reason other than that they seemed like fun. It was partly for its entertainment value that the whole of Chapter Thirteen was translated[8] — the other reason was to expose the patchy time-coverage of past events which was doubtless dictated by the infrequent revision of the gazetteer. To some extent, then, the choice of translation material has been as arbitrary as was the compilation of the original, but the attempt has been made to include a representative coverage of the gazetteer's contents.

The first part of the book consists of a topical treatment of the major subjects covered by the gazetteer. Reference is made to the relevant translations (*T.*) which form the second part, and to standard works which help to place these specific examples in the broad framework of sinological studies.

For those who wish to go direct to the original material, there are two editions of the *Xin'an xianzhi* extant. A copy of the earlier one, dated 1688, is in Beijing, and microfilm copies of this have been made available to the libraries of the University of Hong Kong and the School of Oriental and African Studies, University of London. Barnett lists four even earlier editions,[9] but no copies are known to exist. Copies of the 1819 edition are not uncommon. The University of Hong Kong Library has both the original printed version and a faithful hand-copied version. There was a reprint issued in 1933 without maps, a photographic reprint (also without maps) made in 1974 in Taiwan, and most recently a completely reset edition produced in 1979 by the *Neutral Post* 中立報 in Hong Kong. This last again omits the maps, but supplies a photocopy of the 1866 Volonteri map of Xin'an, the first reasonably accurate map of the region.[10]

It is the 1974 Taiwan reprint which is most readily available, and all page references in this book are to this edition, which is numbered consecutively through the two volumes. For the sake of clarity the maps have been redrawn from the Hong Kong University Library's copies, and also included in the map section are redrawn versions of the 1688 edition maps. A list of the contents of the 1688 edition has been appended for comparison with that of the fuller 1819 edition.

Romanization of Chinese terms is always a problem. In this case all romanization is in the Chinese government *Hanyu pinyin* system 漢語拼音, even where it disguises familiar names (Guangzhou = Canton, Beijing = Peking). But some older spellings are so well established in Hong Kong that it has not seemed proper to change them: thus Hong Kong itself, Kowloon, Punti, Tanka, Hakka, Hoklo, Lantau and Macau are *not* referred to as Xianggang, Jiulong, Bendi, Danjia, Kejia, Fulao, Dayu Shan and Aomen. The Glossary at the back converts the *Pinyin* romanizations of all place names in Hong Kong into the approved Hong Kong Government Cantonese versions. For ease of reading the Chinese word *juan* 卷 has not been romanized where it refers to sections of the Xin'an gazetteer; instead the English word 'chapter' has been used throughout.

A second problem is that of dates. It is tedious and not very helpful to translate Chinese dates too literally. The layman receives little enlightenment from 'the 1st year of the Kangxi reign', and even the specialist will have to go to his reference tables to discover which year of the Western calendar that was. Yet it is not strictly accurate to translate that date as 'AD 1662', because while it began in 1662 it did not end until 7 February 1663. None the less the rough equation is good enough for most purposes, and it is this latter method which is used here. Where a month is given in the text the device of showing both Western months which might apply is used: thus 'the 9th month of the 1st year of the Kangxi reign' would be translated 'September/October 1662' as the 9th month of that year ran from 23 September to 22 October. When specific days are mentioned, an accurate Western date can be given by consulting the concordance tables of Xue and Ouyang.[11]

The following annotated translation of the Table of Contents of the 1819 gazetteer can be referred to for both a summary of and a guide to the body of this book:

TABLE OF CONTENTS OF THE 1819 EDITION OF THE GAZETTEER

Wang Chongxi, Shu Maoguan *et al.* 王崇熙， 舒懋官等(comp.), *Xin'an xianzhi* 新安縣志 [Gazetteer of the Xin'an County], 1819 嘉慶己卯.

	CONTENTS	NOTES
p.1	*Prefatory Material* 序	
	Prefaces: by Ruan Yuan, Viceroy of Guangdong and Guangxi.	Undated preface, but presumably written in 1818 or 1819. Ruan held this office 1817-26. A famous scholar and official whose interest in local history was well known. See Hummel, *Eminent Chinese of the Ch'ing Period*, pp.399-402.
	by Lu Yuanwei, Grain Intendant for Guangdong and Inspecting Intendant for the Southern Marches of Guangzhou Fu.	Preface dated 1818.

	CONTENTS	NOTES
	by Shu Maoguan, County Magistrate of Xin'an.	Preface dated May/June 1819. Shu held the office twice, being appointed in 1816 and 1818.
	by Wang Chongxi.	Preface dated June/July 1819. Wang was general editor of this revised edition.
	Names of those responsible for revising the gazetteer	A general editor, six assistant editors, and five consultant compilers, all under the supervision of the County Magistrate.
	Notes on the revision of the gazetteer	See translation passage *T.1*.
	Contents of the revised gazetteer	Headings and subheads of the twenty-five chapters.
p.17	*Premier Chapter* 卷首 — *Imperial edicts* 訓典	A collection of thirty-two edicts relevant to the county's interests, the earliest dated 1652, the latest 1819. See *T.2*, *T.3*, *T.4*, *T.5*, *T.6*, *T.7*, *T.8*, *T.9*.
P.65	*Chapter One — History* 沿革志	
	Table of the county's history 沿革表	A concise outline of the changes of name and administration since earliest times. See *T.10*.
	Annexe: further detail 考附	
p.71	*Chapter Two — Topography (1)* 輿地略一	
	Maps 輿圖	Of the county, of Xin'an and Dapeng cities, and of the

CONTENTS	NOTES
	coastal defences. (See Maps 3, 4, 5 and 6). Not reproduced in the Cheng Wen edition or in the *Neutral Post* edition.
Boundaries 疆域	See *T.11.*
Geographical position 分野	Xin'an's position on a grid system where earthly and heavenly phenomena are made to correspond. See Needham, *Science and Civilization in China*, vol.3, p.545.
Climate 氣候	
Annexe: wind-lore 風異附	See *T.12.*
Guangdong Province month by month 月令	A brief naturalist's diary.
Annexe: weather-lore 占候附	Popular sayings of the 'red sky at night, shepherd's delight' type.
Customs 風俗	See *T.13.*
Markets 墟市	A list of all thirty-six of the county's markets, plus four defunct markets and one transferred to Dongguan County.
Villages 都里	Names of the county's villages arranged into the areas presided over by the various officials, and subdivided into 'Cantonese' and 'Hakka' categories. See *T.14.*

	CONTENTS	NOTES
p.121	*Chapter Three — Topography (2)* 輿地略二	
	Products 物產 Grains Vegetables Teas Fruits Flowers Herbs Trees Bamboos Rattans Birds Animals Fish Shellfish Insects and pests	Under each subhead are listed the names of the various products. For most of them brief descriptions and notes on their uses are given.
p.141	*Chapter Four — Scenic features* 山水略	The names and locations of the principal landmarks of the county.
	Mountains	Ninety-five entries subdivided into mountains, peaks, ridges, passes and valleys. See *T.15.*
	Waters 水	Thirty-nine entries subdivided into seas, straits, rivers, bays, islands, pools and streams. See *T.16.*
	Annexe: reservoirs and dams 陂堰附	Sixteen entries.
	Tides 潮汐	The seasonal variations in the tides and the local names for them.
	Wells and springs 井泉	Sixteen entries.

	CONTENTS	NOTES
p.161	*Chapter Five — Officials (1)* 職官志一	
	Civil establishment 文官制	See *T.17*.
	Military establishment 武官制	The officers of the two battalions stationed at Xin'an and Dapeng. See *T.30* where the information is duplicated.
	List of civil officials 文官表	The names, counties of origin, academic qualifications and year of taking office of all holders of civil office in the county since its inception in 1573. The data for some officials are incomplete. Pages 190-91 are missing from the Cheng Wen edition.
p.209	*Chapter Six — Officials (2)* 職官志二	
	List of military officials 武官表	As for civil officials, but usually only the province of origin given, and very few military qualifications are noted.
p.241	*Chapter Seven — Buildings* 建置略	
	Walled and moated cities 城池 Xin'an City 邑城 Dapeng City 大鵬所城	See *T.18*. Names of streets, parade grounds, and other city features are also given.
	Government offices 廨署	The location of the civil and military buildings, with a very full description of the County Magistrate's yamen and briefer notes on the rest. See *T.19*.

	CONTENTS	NOTES
		The *Xiangshe* 鄉射 archery contest. Books received by the education authorities between 1723 and 1815; student quotas; special quotas for Hakka people: see *T.25*. Land rents to finance education.
	Academies 書院	The defunct Wengang Academy; the Fenggang Academy, its lands and rental income. See *T.26*.
	Charity schools 義學	Seven schools, one functioning, one converted to a temple, the rest defunct.
p.315	*Chapter Ten — Administration (3)* 經政略三	
	Ceremonial 禮制	Instructions to officials about observances for the birthdays of the Emperor and Empress; on receiving Imperial edicts; at the *Xiangyue* lectures: see *T.27*; on eclipses: see *T.28*; at the coming of spring; on first taking office; and at twice-monthly temple worship. See *T.29*.
	Worship 祀典	Details of the tablets installed in the Temple for Civil Rites; offerings; ritual paraphernalia; musical instruments; and order of services.
p.347	*Chapter Eleven — Administration (4)* 經政略四	
	Military system 兵制	The garrisons and their staffing: see *T.30*; signal stations; dyke

CONTENTS	NOTES
p.393 *Chapter Fifteen — Preferment (1)* 選擧表一	
Recommended to the throne 薦辟	One man who in 1382 was appointed to a post by recommendation rather than by examination. At that time this was a common practice: indeed between 1373 and 1384 no examinations were held. See Hucker, 'Government Organization of the Ming Dynasty', pp.70-71.
Jinshi 甲科 *Juren* 鄉科 *Bagongsheng* 拔貢 *Yougongsheng* 優貢 *Engongsheng* 恩貢 *Suigongsheng* 歲貢	The names of men of the county who passed the various civil service examinations, the dates when they passed, and posts (if any) which they eventually held. For the differences between these degrees see Mayers, *The Chinese Government*, pp.76-83 and Ch'ü, *Local Government in China under the Ch'ing*, p.317.
Civil postings attained without higher degree 文職不由科貢者	Five entries.
p.423 *Chapter Sixteen — Preferment (2)* 選擧表二	
Military *jinshi* 武甲科 Military *juren* 武鄉科	Similar information to the above, but for passers of military examinations.
Military postings 武職	111 men appointed to military posts without formal degrees.

	CONTENTS	NOTES
	Men of loyalty and righteousness 忠義	Five entries. See *T.41b*.
	Men of loyalty and courage 忠勇	Six entries. See *T.41c*.
	Annexe: chivalrous men 義俠附	One entry.
	Recluses 隱逸	Four entries.
p.497	*Chapter Twenty — Notable people (2)* 人物志二	
	Women of heroic virtue 列女傳	Short notes on eleven women who chose death rather than dishonour, or who remained chaste in the face of hardship. See *T.42a*.
	Lifelong virgins (officially honoured) 貞女	Twenty-four names. See *T.42b*.
	Chaste widows (officially honoured) 節婦	Sixty-six names. See *T.42c*.
	Lifelong virgins	Forty-eight names. See *T.42d*.
	Chaste widows	248 names. See *T.42e*.
	Chaste widows (Hakka) 客籍節婦	Three names.
p.535	*Chapter Twenty-one — Notable people (3)* 人物志三	
	Long-lived men 壽考	Eleven men who reached the age of ninety-eight and above. See *T.43a*.
	Long-lived women 壽婦	Three women of ninety-nine and above. See *T.43b*.
	Sojourners 流寓	Four men who came to the county from elsewhere. See *T.43c*.

Part One

1. History
2. Geography
3. Economy
4. Government

1. HISTORY

Chinese civilization developed in the basin of the Yellow River and spread only slowly to fill the enormous area of more than 3,600,000 square miles which is present-day China. Long before it reached as far south as Hong Kong the area was inhabited by other peoples. Present evidence points to coastal settlements dating back to about 3000 BC,[1] but archaeological research in Hong Kong has been gaining momentum in recent years and the picture may change as more discoveries are made.[2]

In the 13th year of King Wu of Zhou 周武王 south China was proclaimed a tributary state 藩服 [3] from which it may be assumed that some of the aboriginal tribes might have sent tribute or trading missions to the capitals of various feudal states.

The Yue 越 people, classified as palaeo-Austronesian,[4] occupied the maritime south-east from about the sixth century BC to Han 漢 times when they became sinicized,[5] but other non-Chinese were probably there at the same time, and they and others who migrated in later were much in evidence until about a thousand years ago. Even today Guangdong Province still contains Yao 猺, Zhuang 僮, Miao 苗, Li 黎, She 畲 and Jing 京 minority peoples.[6]

The region was brought under Chinese rule for the first time by Shihuangdi 始皇帝, the first emperor of China and founder of the Qin 秦 dynasty. His armies penetrated to the south in 234 and 222 BC and the area they partially subjugated was divided into three departments 郡, one of which, Nan Hai 南海, roughly corresponded to Guangdong Province of later times.[7] The conquest was undertaken as a stage in the wider project for the political unification of China which finally brought the era of the Warring States 戰國 to an end in 221 BC. But the administration of south China was left semi-independent, with powerful military governors only nominally responsible to the imperial government. When the Qin dynasty collapsed in 207 BC., one of the military governors, Zhao Tuo 趙佗, amalgamated the three departments into one and set himself up as King of Nan Yue 南越 changing the name Nan Hai to Nan Wu 南武 in 196 BC.[8] His domain extended over the land which now forms the provinces of Guangdong and Guangxi.[9]

The kingdom stood for nearly a century during which time tribute was sent regularly to the Chinese capital. In 111 BC it fell under the pressure exerted by the Han dynasty, which was completing the work of unification that had been set on foot by the Qin. South China was again divided into departments and subdivided into counties. Nan Hai had six counties and of these it was the county of Boluo 博羅 which controlled our area. From the Han dynasty onwards the names of the administrative units changed through Bao'an 寶安 and Dongguan 東莞 to the creation of Xin'an County in 1573.[10]

To the relatively sophisticated northern Chinese of Han times the south was a wild and fearsome place. A contemporary description of the peoples of the area shows how alien they were felt to be:

> ...cutting the hair short, tattooing the body, possessing neither towns nor villages but living in valleys of bamboo, expert at fishing but of no use on land, having neither chariots nor horses nor bows and arrows.[11]

The colonization of south China had begun with the transportation of convicts from the north to open up waste-land and the posting of garrisons at strategic points along the border. But a combination of climate, disease and unfriendly inhabitants made the area a most inhospitable one. Wiens calls it a 'kind of tropical "Siberia"'. The Chinese tended to be restricted to cities and major settlements; they

> moved into the rich valleys of the south in 'pools' — dense aggregations of hopeful humanity, supported by troops who killed those natives bold enough to resist, leaving the survivors to be indoctrinated, exploited or enslaved by Chinese agents and their aboriginal collaborators.[12]

This military colonization was carried on by other dynasties, but implemented most strongly during the Tang dynasty. The establishing of the Tang in AD 618 marked the beginning of an important period in the history of south China. Intercourse with foreign nations was actively encouraged by the government, and with the growth of foreign trade Guangzhou acquired considerable importance as a commercial centre. Arabs, Indians and Persians came, and Chinese junks also appeared at the ports of South-east Asia and India. In course of time the amount of trade assumed such proportions that the government felt justified in sending a Commissioner of Shipping to Guangzhou to supervise the collection of customs revenue.[13]

With growing prosperity and heavy Chinese immigration into the province the Tang period came to be considered a golden age for Guangdong. Even today the Cantonese refer to themselves as 'People of the Tang' 唐人, to the Chinese language as the 'Language of the Tang' 唐話 and to China as the 'Land of the Tang' 唐山.[14]

It is in Tang sources that we find the first mention of a settlement in the Hong Kong region. A garrison 鎮 was appointed at Tunmen 屯門 to stand guard over the mouth of the Pearl River 珠江 through which so many Chinese and foreign ships passed.[15] With its conspicuous peak and natural harbour Tunmen was probably a place where foreign ships would anchor for supplies and to conduct trading negotiations. It is mentioned in the official history of the Tang dynasty.:

> Sailing from Guangzhou towards the south-east for 200 *li* one reaches Mount Tunmen.[16]

The same landmark is referred to in a description of a storm in a poem by the celebrated Han Yu 韓愈 (AD 768-824):

> Though Tunmen is considered high, 屯門雖云高
> The waves have swallowed it up. 亦映波濤沒[17]

Han Yu may never have actually visited the spot, but the stone inscription 'Greatest of High Mountains' 高山第一 which is found there has traditionally been attributed to him. The stone is above the monastery founded by the Buddhist monk Beidu 杯渡 some two hundred years before Han Yu's time. A detailed description of the monastery is given in the gazetteer.[18]

The fall of the Tang dynasty in 906 was followed by widespread civil strife. For more than half a century China was divided among many petty states. Guangdong came under the rule of local kings who gave their dynasty the name of Southern Han 南漢. Under them our area achieved notoriety as a centre for the pearl-fishing industry, one of the chief sources of pearls being a place called Meichuan 媚川 or Meizhuchi 媚珠池 which has been identified as Tolo Harbour 大埔海 on the east side of the present New Territories:

> Liu Chang 劉鋹 [the last Southern Han King] occupied Ling Nan 嶺南 and recruited eight thousand men for the specific purpose of gathering pearls at Meichuan Dou 媚川都. Each man had a stone tied to his foot and had to dive to a depth of five to seven hundred feet. Drownings were commonplace. In due course his treasuries became so well stored with pearls that the pillars and curtains of his palace were all decorated with them and were extremely magnificent.[19]

The Song dynasty, to which Liu Chang's Southern Han fell in 971, abolished the pearl-fishing, but it was revived at various times up until the late seventeenth century when it became clear that the beds were worked out and uneconomic.[20]

In history there have been two major movements of the Chinese people southwards. The first occurred in the early fourth century AD as a result of famine and invasion from the north by the Wu Hu 五胡 tribes. It pushed tens of thousands of Chinese down to the Yangtze basin. The second mass migration came eight hundred years later when the Song dynasty was forced, again by barbarian invasion, to relocate its capital in the south, and large numbers of people fled into areas previously only nominally Chinese. It was during this second phase that Guangdong, Fujian and Guangxi provinces were settled on a large scale[21] and for the first time much of the land of our area (at that time called Dongguan County) came under the Chinese plough.

The Yao who then lived in the Hong Kong region were either absorbed or annihilated when the Chinese settlers moved in. They had presumably practised the same 'slash-and-burn' 刀耕火耨 shifting agriculture as other Yao tribes and it has been suggested that the continuing practice of setting fire to hillsides in the New Territories might be a legacy of this aboriginal technique.[22] Some scanty evidence for their early contact with the Chinese settlers comes from linguistic sources. Barnett has said:

> It is quite certain that the *Yao* were one of the two pre-Chinese people living on the hills of this territory: and it is almost a certainty that many of our present inhabitants are their descendants.[23]

As support for his point he has compiled lists of allegedly 'non-Chinese' words which appear in local place names,[24] and has shown how in some cases these tie in with terms recorded in the Tang dynasty work the *Manshu* 蠻書 ,[25] which deals with minority peoples in Yunnan. The other aboriginal people referred to by Barnett are the Shanliao 山獠 , but he can produce no real proof of their existence. Another researcher, Lim Tien-wai, has mustered plenty of evidence for the existence of Yao tribesmen on Lantau Island near Hong Kong, and he believes that some trace of them was probably still there until towards the end of the Ming dynasty, but he managed to find no positive proof of a Shanliao presence either.[26]

The Dan 蜑 , people probably of the same stock as the Yao, specialized in a life on water.[27] They became the ancestors of the boat-dwelling peoples of Guangdong and Fujian provinces, and their name survives in the Hong Kong region where the boat people are known as the Danjia 蜑家 (commonly romanized 'Tanka'). Yao culture in the Hong Kong area was swamped by the stronger Chinese culture: the Dan may have survived longer as a distinct cultural group, but it is clear that they have for long now also been sinicized.[28] They speak a dialect of Cantonese and resent the pejorative implication of 'uncivilized' which the term Danjia carries with it.[29] They refer to themselves as 'water-borne people' 水上人 or 'people of the Tang' 唐人 (a regular Cantonese term for 'Chinese', as we have seen) and cannot now be seriously considered as non-Chinese.

Most of the land which the Chinese settlers were moving into was unbroken and the hills were probably heavily forested:[30]

> Much of the country must have been jungle. The presence of elephants is shown by an inscription dated AD 962 at a Buddhist temple not far from the present frontier. The inscription describes the erection of a pagoda on a site where elephant bones were collected and buried in order to pacify herds of elephants which were doing great damage in the neighbourhood....We have already seen that crocodiles were common in South China during the T'ang dynasty.[31]

Among the first Chinese settlers in the district were a family surnamed Deng 鄧 whose descendants are still probably the largest landowners in the New Territories today. Their genealogy, compiled in the Ming dynasty, reveals that the founder of the Xin'an branch, Deng Fuxie 鄧符協, was originally a native of Jiangxi Province. He held the *jinshi* degree and in AD 973[32] passed through Guangdong on his way to take up an official post. Much taken with the area, he chose upon retirement to settle at Jintian 錦田 where he built two villages on the sites where the New Territories villages of Beiwei 北圍 and Nanwei 南圍 stand today.

Deng Fuxie by accident or design had selected highly fertile well-watered land. Very quickly the Deng prospered and expanded to dominate the Jintian plain; and then over the course of some three hundred years they sent offshoots to colonize nearby areas and further afield into other counties.[33] In the early years of the Southern Song dynasty a Deng from Jintian gave assistance to and then married the daughter of the emperor Gaozong 高宗 (reigned 1127-62). Deng is said to have been unaware of her identity at first, but when the marriage was finally recognized by the emperor gifts of land and tax rights were given to the bride by her father, swelling the fortunes of the Deng and making their continued prosperity certain.[34]

The ancestors of other major surnames of the New Territories also arrived on the scene at around this time. The island of Lantau was granted to the Li 李 family in the early thirteenth century, though they never farmed or lived on it themselves.[35] The Hou 侯 lineage of Heshangxiang 河上鄉 and the Peng 彭 of Fenling 粉嶺 were founded in the twelfth and thirteenth centuries respectively, and in the century after the collapse of the Song in 1279 the Liao 廖 of Shangshui 上水 and the Wen 文 of Xintian 新田 and Taikeng 泰坑 had settled in the area.[36] The local evidence seems to bear out F.L. Wong's statement:

> Generally speaking, the historical movement of the people of the Central Plain into Guangdong was at its greatest at the end of the Song and beginning of the Yuan. From that time onward Cantonese culture was raised to a high level under the influences brought to the south by the Central Plainsmen; indeed it might be said that the two cultures became equally great.[37]

Farming was the chief but not the only occupation of the region. Of Lantau Island during the Song the provincial gazetteer says:

> the inhabitants neither farm nor make silk, nor do they pay taxes or do labour service. They live by fishing and salt making.[38]

An attempt in 1197 to stop private trading in salt led to the revolt of the islanders who successfully repulsed a government invasion force by mining their harbours with wooden stakes and then fighting a sea battle (at which they excelled). Getting over-eager they then sailed up to Guangzhou, but were defeated by the tactics of the navy whose sailors jumped aboard them to cut their sails and make them helpless, then fired rockets to finish them off. This action is thought to have been the end of Yao domination of Lantau, the survivors fleeing or becoming absorbed by the Chinese.[39]

Much sentimental value has been attached to the story of the journey of the last Song emperors through the region, and many legends have been woven around this theme. When the emperor Gongdi 恭帝 was taken prisoner at Lin'an 臨安 by Mongol forces in 1276, his two brothers, the Prince of Yi 益王 and the Prince of Guang 廣王 , fled with their mothers and loyal ministers to Fuzhou 福州 , where the Prince of Yi was declared emperor. When Fuzhou was threatened by the Mongol troops, they made their way into Guangdong Province. Unable to find refuge at Guangzhou because enemy pressure was being focused on it, the travelling court entered our region in early 1277, and at first settled on the by then fully pacified island of Lantau, at Meiwei 梅蔚 (now known as Meiwo 梅窩). Afterwards they moved to the Kowloon peninsula, where the emperor set up his court near Kowloon City at the place where the Songwangtai 宋王臺 stood until its recent demolition. When he died in 1278, his eight-year-old brother was proclaimed emperor. But the Mongol forces closed in inexorably, forcing the court to flee to Xinhui County 新會縣 where in 1279 the emperor and his chief ministers are said to have committed suicide by leaping into the sea.[40]

Traces of the imperial sojourn may still be found in present-day Hong Kong, among them the stone carved with the three characters 宋王臺 and the Houwang 侯王 temple at Kowloon. 'Houwang' is thought to be the posthumous title of the emperors' uncle, Yang Liangjie 楊亮節 . Throughout the difficult period he devoted himself to the protection of his imperial wards and to planning for their restoration, and when he died the local inhabitants are said to have erected the temple to his memory.[41]

A result of this tragic period was that much of the Song army probably settled in the region after their final defeat, thus increasing the population of the county and contributing to its development. One of the ministers taking a leading part in the campaigns in south China against the Mongols was Wen Tianxiang 文天祥 (1236-83), and the Wen lineages of Xintian and Taikeng in the New Territories claim descent from this hero who died a martyr's death in Beijing. The old village of Matouwei 馬頭圍 (now part of Kowloon) was inhabited by the Zhao 趙 lineage until towards the end of the Qing 清 dynasty. Zhao was the surname of the Song imperial family, from whom this lineage are said to have descended.[42]

The Mongol conquest and founding of the Yuan 元 dynasty in 1280 did not bring peace to the area for long. Rebellions broke out repeatedly[43] and when in 1368 the Mongols were finally ousted by Zhu Yuanzhang 朱元璋 who founded the Ming 明 dynasty, Guangdong was handed over without bloodshed by its commander He Zhen 何眞 who was a native of our area. He was rewarded with the title Earl of Dongguan 東莞伯 , the name which the county then bore.[44]

During the Ming dynasty the peaceful colonization of the region went on its way. But the arrival of the Portuguese in the early sixteenth century made military defence an urgent problem for the Ming government. As Guangzhou was still the centre of foreign trade, Tunmen at the mouth of the Pearl River remained an important anchorage. It was visited by the first Portuguese to arrive in China, Jorge Alvares, who placed a *padrão*[45] there in 1513 and who was in fact buried there upon his death during a later voyage to China in 1521.[46] The Portuguese fully understood the possibilities of Tunmen, which commanded the entrance and exit of ships using the Pearl River and where a settlement would enable them to dominate the foreign trade. Thus when Simão Peres de Andrade reached China in 1519 he built a fort in the neighbourhood of Tunmen without first seeking Chinese government permission. This and other tactless behaviour was resented by the Chinese, and in 1521 a Chinese naval force fell on the Portuguese and defeated them.[47]

> In 1522 another expedition set sail from Malacca. They were met outside T'un Mun by a large Chinese fleet and although they did not at first return the fire and tried to open negotiations they were chased to the western side of the Canton estuary near San Wui district where another battle took place in which they were all killed or captured....The Chinese had by that time under the energetic leadership of Wang Hung learnt to make cannon after the Portuguese model and were

> not any more at a disadvantage in this respect. But after the last Portuguese defeat the region of T'un Mun was left alone. A Chinese fleet patrolled the estuary and the islands continually from 1523 to 1524 but the foreigners did not reappear for many years.[48]

Another reason for the strengthening of the coastal defences was the continual presence of Chinese and Japanese pirates (the latter being known as *Wokou* 倭寇 'Dwarf Pirates'). Nantou 南頭 was the base of the *Beiwo tuzhihui* 備倭土指揮 (?) (Local Commander of Forces for the Defence against Japanese Pirates),[49] and in 1586 it was considered necessary for a Brigadier-General 總兵 to have his headquarters transferred there also, so that he could 'control the barbarians and the dwarfs'.[50]

The prevalence of piracy and the threat of a 'barbarian' invasion led to an important development in the administration of our area, which had been part of Dongguan County since AD 757. It was proposed that it should be severed from Dongguan and turned into a separate county, so that it could be controlled and defended more easily. The proposal was accepted by the central government, and in 1573 Xin'an County 新安縣 had its birth as an administrative unit with its county town at Nantou.

But pirates continued to infest the coast and the problem grew in magnitude in the last days of the Ming.[51] Geographical conditions seem to have helped to make Xin'an a breeding ground for piracy: it stands along the rich and busy route to Guangzhou and has an irregular coastline, with innumerable islands providing ideal places for hiding.

For the first twenty-five years of the Qing dynasty, piracy was such a menace that orders were eventually given for the coastal populations of Guangdong, Fujian, Zhejiang, Jiangsu and Shandong provinces to be evacuated inland. The official reason was to protect the population from piratical incursions, but the real purpose was to prevent the powerful naval forces of the Ming loyalist Zheng Chenggong 鄭成功 (known to the West as Koxinga) from having access to supplies and support. This 'scorched earth' policy is thought to have been proposed by Huang Wu 黃梧, one of Koxinga's officers who had gone over to the government side.[52]

The evacuation of Xin'an began in 1662 when the people were ordered to move behind a boundary which had been set up fifty *li* from the coast. At first there was a tendency to ignore the decree and soldiers had to be marched in to enforce it. When the people had been driven away, a chain of fortifications was set up along the coast. Two years later another evacuation took place, the boundary being placed further inland. According to the gazetteer the original plan was to evacuate the whole of Xin'an, but the Governor-General petitioned for leniency, and eventually only twenty-four more villages in the east and west were evacuated.[53]

Terrible suffering must have ensued. Hsieh quotes a Chinese account of evacuation from nearby counties:

> The boundary was marked straight with a rope, so that sometimes one house or even one room was divided into halves, one half on the outside and the other half on the inside of the line. A deep ditch was dug to serve as the boundary; one step beyond the ditch, and the punishment was death. Those who were removed had to leave their houses and property, wandering about without support.[54]

Qu Dajun's description is even more graphic:

> At first the evacuees thought they would soon be able to return and could not bring themselves to part from their own flesh and blood; but as time went by and they continued to drift around, they could not support themselves Fathers abandoned their sons and husbands their wives, agonizing separations. Sons were sold for a peck of rice, daughters for a hundred cash .... The young men went off to become soldiers, the aged and weak slept in ditches. Some families took poison *en masse*, others jumped in the river when their funds were exhausted. The authorities treated the people as no more than ants and made no provision for relief; relatives treated each other as mere dirt and did not observe the niceties of dutiful behaviour. It is reckoned that several hundred thousand people from the eight departments affected died. Since the people had all been evacuated, their houses were demolished to provide materials for building fortifications, and their graves were dug up to make deep moats. Every five *li* there was a beacon, and every ten *li* a watch-tower.[55]

In 1666 the depleted county was once more merged with Dongguan, and it was not restored to independent status until 1669 when, as a result of strong pressure from the Governor of Guangdong Wang Lairen 王來任 and from the Governor-General Zhou Youde 周有德, the evacuation order was lifted and those people who survived were able to return to their homelands.[56]

The grateful few built temples to commemorate and worship Wang and Zhou. The gazetteer mentions three of them in Xin'an under the heading 王巡撫祠 (Governor Wang Halls),[57] and a fourth still survives at Jintian in the New Territories.[58] Probably the building of houses to replace the demolished old ones took priority over the temples, for the 1688 edition of the gazetteer mentions none of them.

The population figures for Xin'an given in the gazetteer are certainly not to be accepted as accurate, but they probably reflect in degree the pattern. From

17,871 people in 1642 just prior to the collapse of the Ming dynasty the numbers sank to a total of 2,172 males remaining after the two evacuations, and by 1672, three years after the reoccupation, a total population of only 3,972 is reported.[59]

Meanwhile tax revenue had fallen heavily, for agriculture and the salt production industry had both run down, and the old trade in incense had disappeared completely. This last is supposed to have given Hong Kong its name 香港 'Incense Port': certainly it seems a more likely derivation than the common translation 'Fragrant Harbour'.[60] Positive attempts were made by the government to repopulate the county, and as elsewhere in Guangdong Province it was to the disadvantaged Hakka 客家 people that they turned.[61] Hakka settlers came in to take up whatever land had not been claimed by the original Cantonese-speaking inhabitants (the Punti 本地) when they returned. A pattern of settlement was created by this which remained down to the twentieth century: the large fertile plains were more or less monopolized by the major Cantonese-speaking lineages, and the more inaccessible, higher and less fertile lands were taken up by the Hakka or by Cantonese families who arrived late on the scene.[62] Even so not all land was settled to the government's satisfaction.[63]

The evacuation did not put an end to the practice of piracy in Xin'an. In the early years of the nineteenth century the most prominent pirate in the region was Zhang Baozi 張保仔, who is said to have commanded over two hundred and fifty junks and to have had some forty thousand followers. He successfully defied the Qing government until along with other pirate chiefs he surrendered in 1810. Hong Kong and other nearby islands had served as his main base, and after his surrender the local inhabitants changed the name of Hong Kong's highest peak from Yingtou Shan 硬頭山 to Taiping Shan 太平山 or Peaceful Mountain, the name by which Victoria Peak is still known to the Chinese today.[64] Strangely Zhang's name does not appear in the gazetteer.

From 1819 when this last edition of the gazetteer was produced the history of Xin'an becomes more and more concerned with the encroaching West. In 1842 the island of Hong Kong was ceded to the British Crown. The developments which led to the birth of the Colony had their origin in the China trade and are outside the scope of this work,[65] but together with what can be taken as their logical sequels — the cession of Kowloon in 1860 and the lease of the New Territories in 1898 — they were to change radically the way of life of the bulk of Xin'an's inhabitants.

2. GEOGRAPHY

The county of Xin'an as it stood before the cession of territory to the British Crown had a total area of something under 600 square miles. To the west of it is the wide estuary of the Pearl River which brings down mud from Guangdong Province and by depositing it along the coast creates a good deal of flat plain; to its south and south-east is the sea, with a long fringe of islands off the coast; and to its north is the prosperous Dongguan County.

In terms of China's long history, in terms of wealth of local products, and in terms of population size and composition Xin'an was of no particular importance. Only in its strategic position at the mouth of the Pearl River did it have much significance for the Chinese government, and geographical information in the gazetteer is accordingly less than comprehensive.

Physical

Physically the region is composed of two fairly distinct areas. The northern half, bordered by Dongguan and Guixin 歸善縣 counties and girded in the south by a line of hills running from Deep Bay north-eastwards, is low-lying country with conditions favourable to agriculture. The southern half is a large peninsula jutting into the sea and surrounded by numerous irregularly-shaped islands. With the exception of Kowloon, this part of the county is quite rugged, especially in the Mirs Bay region, and useful land is scarce. For instance, only some 13 per cent of the land area of the New Territories is capable of cultivation.[1]

The climate is characterized by a dry, cool north-east monsoon in winter and a hot, humid south-west monsoon in summer. On average 90 per cent of the annual rainfall occurs in the summer months from April to October,[2] and much of that may come from typhoons.[3] Many of the hills are badly eroded where alternate sunbaking and torrential rainfall have stripped the topsoil away. Water retention is minimal and drought can occur very shortly after abundant rain, but on sheltered hillsides and in the valleys vegetation is lush.

Chapter Three of the gazetteer lists a great variety of vegetable products of the area, including some thirty different grains, many green vegetables, teas, bamboos, rattans, and sub-tropical fruits such as litchis, pomelos, water-melons and pineapples. Tigers, monkeys, deer, wild boar, otters and several kinds of snake are noted as native residents, and the importance of the sea is stressed by the inclusion of thirty-five different types of fish as well as various shellfish.

In the 1688 edition of the gazetteer the information on Xin'an's territory is very sketchy. Not only does the 1819 edition have to correct the measurements of the size of the county, but it points out that the islands off the coast have been left out of the old reckoning and should now be included.[4]

The two maps of 1688 are not much more helpful than the text. The map of Xin'an City (Map 2) is a highly stylized and very uninformative picture of a city wall with four gates. The subsidiary wall at the east gate is not shown, and only a handful of features such as the county yamen, the Guandi Temple and the Temple for Civil Rites are picked out for inclusion. The map of the county (Map 1) is only a representation of the territory in the broadest sense. Neither perspective nor scale nor a serious attempt to show the geographical layout of the county is in evidence. The county seat is shown large at the centre of the map and all else is subordinated to it.

The Xin'an City map of 1819 (Map 4) includes more detail such as buildings inside and around the walls, and even shows the two sluice gates, but the landscape into which it is set is stylized and far from accurate. Some of the blanks for naming geographical features have not been filled in. Map 5 is an equally stylized but less detailed plan of Dapeng City. The map of the county (Map 3) is a considerable improvement over the 1688 map, the county seat and Dapeng being shown in more or less the correct positions, while a much larger number of other place names and the approximate positions of the old subdistricts of the county are given. Still the representation of the physical landscape and of the coastline is crude and out of proportion. The islands are undifferentiated by size or shape, some are wrongly positioned, and carelessness as to accuracy results in some features being misrepresented — for example, the highest mountain in Hong Kong's mainland territory (Damao Shan 大帽山) is shown as an island.

Much the same may be said of the coastal defence map (Map 6), which shows the many forts and guard-posts placed around the county's shores. It could certainly not be used as a navigator's chart, islands being scattered throughout the large area of sea with scant regard for true size or position. For the first time the island of Hong Kong appears on a Chinese map under the name Hongxianglu 紅香爐,[5] but the settlement of Stanley 赤柱 is shown as a separate island to the south of Hong Kong, and a third island labelled Xiaoyiwan 校椅灣 which separates the two may or may not represent the fishing village of Shaojiwan 筲箕灣 on Hong Kong's north-eastern shore. To add confusion the coastline differs in shape from that of Map 3.

Chapter Four 'Scenic Features' contains a large number of entries under its various headings, but it is quite undiscriminating in its treatment, mixing major rivers and mountains with insignificant streams and knolls. Probably the inclusion of any one feature was dictated more by its familiarity to the particular compilers of the gazetteer than by its objective importance.[6] The positions of the named landmarks are given with reference to the county seat or other known places, thus:

> Daxi Shan 大奚山, otherwise known as Dayu Shan 大嶼山 [i.e. Lantau Island], is more than 100 *li* south of the county seat and separates Jishuimen 急水門 from Fotangmen 佛堂門.[7]

Alternatively a less specific reference to the *Dou* 都 in which they were to be found is given thus:

> Daguling 打鼓嶺 is in the sixth *Dou* and popular legend has it that the sound of drums can be heard there on windy rainy nights.

Political

The *Dou* was one of the subdistricts into which the county was divided. According to the 1688 gazetteer Xin'an comprised three *Xiang* 鄉, seven *Dou*, fifty-seven *Tu* 啚 and five hundred *Cun* 村. Endexiang 恩德鄉 was split between the first, second and third *Dou*, while the fourth and fifth *Dou* made up Yanfuxiang 延福鄉, and the sixth and seventh *Dou* shared Guichengxiang 歸城鄉.[8] Divisions such as these were created for taxation purposes, different counties adopting a bewildering variety of names for them.[9] Yet, other than in the map of the county and such locational reference as the above, the 1819 edition nowhere indicates that the *Xiang — Dou — Tu — Cun* system was in regular use at that time.[10] The county was divided instead into four administrative areas, the villages of which were further classified as Cantonese (Punti) or Hakka according to the ethnicity of their inhabitants.[11]

The Chief of Police 典史 controlled the area around the county seat, a total of sixty-seven Punti and six Hakka settlements. The Deputy Magistrate 縣丞 was responsible for sixty Punti and forty-four Hakka villages (seven of the latter were apparently unnamed as the gazetteer merely records them as 'Wang surname', 'Zhang surname' etc.). The Guanfu Assistant Magistrate 官富巡檢 was in charge of 301 Punti and 194 Hakka villages in the areas which later came under British rule, and the Fuyong Assistant Magistrate 福永巡檢 had the remaining 154 Punti and 31 Hakka settlements.[12]

The number of villages seems large for a county of this size, but many of the settlements were extremely small. In the Chinese administrative sense a few farmsteads lying close to each other would constitute a *cunzhuang* 村庄 'village', and even the market towns 墟市 were for the most part little more than villages where fairs or markets were regularly held three times every ten-day lunar 'week' 旬.

Maps 7 and 8 reconstruct the divisions of 1688 and 1819 from the given lists of settlements.

The seat of the administration was Xin'an City situated at Nantou in the north-western part of the county. Nantou is a small peninsula dividing Deep Bay from the Pearl River estuary. It was considered most important from the strategic point of view, and was defended by a large fort where was stationed one of the two battalions of troops assigned to the county.[13] Xin'an was probably the largest city in the region: it is described as having twenty-five streets, seventeen of which were outside the walled area,[14] and was important as the seat of the county magistrate's yamen, and the centre of the county civil service examinations.

The other major city which is described in detail is Dapeng 大鵬 in the extreme east above Mirs Bay. Dapeng served as the seat of the Deputy Magistrate and the headquarters of the important Dapeng Battalion.

It is likely that neither of the Assistant Magistrates' headquarters were walled or defended as Xin'an and Dapeng were, though when the Guanfu official's yamen was moved to Kowloon a city wall was built in 1847 to protect it.[15] At a lower level, however, there were many walled settlements which were not administrative centres. Eighty-three of the 857 place names listed in the four divisions end in the word *wei* 圍 'enclosure', a sure sign that the settlement had a wall. Since there were many villages with walls which did not employ *wei* in their name (for example, Shangshuicun 上水村, Longyuetou 龍躍頭, and Heshangxiang 河上鄉[16]) it can be seen that the proportion of protected villages was high. By the nineteenth century the walls were a major feature of interlineage feuding, but in some cases at least they had been built originally to keep out the many bandits and pirates who plagued the area. Those of Shangshui and of two of the Jintian villages, for instance, are known to have been designed to combat the depredations of the 'Ming loyalist forces' of Li Wanrong 李萬榮 in the mid-seventeenth century.[17]

Whether walled or not the common pattern of settlement throughout the county was a tightly-packed group of terraced houses and outbuildings surrounded by the fields which provided the income of the inhabitants. Isolated farmhouses were virtually unknown, only the occasional temple or monastery daring to stand aloof from the (often illusory) safety of the huddled village.

The gazetteer has little to say on standards of housing, merely remarking that plaster and brick had replaced the primitive mud walls of former times.[18] In fact some mud-brick housing is still in evidence today, and in the nineteenth century there was certainly much more, particularly where there were the hereditary servants maintained by the major lineages.[19] Most houses consisted of a single room with an antechamber which served as kitchen and wash-room. A wooden cockloft reached by ladder provided additional sleeping or storage space. Roofs were tiled over wooden beams, no windows were provided, entry could only be gained through the stout, heavily barred front doors: and thus were the residents made safe from both men and spirits who might do them harm. Of the latter all men were afraid and protective charms were permanently displayed at the door.[20]

In addition to houses and pigsties most villages contained one or more temples to Taoist or Buddhist gods, and in many villages there were also ancestral halls maintained out of lineage funds for the worship of the inhabitants' forebears.[21] Hakka halls differed from Punti ones in having just one composite ancestor tablet, the latter installing a separate tablet for every ancestor worshipped.[22]

Human

Despite the gazetteer's careful separation of Punti from Hakka villages and its note of the special examination pass quotas for Hakka men[23] no attempt is made either in the 'Customs' section of Chapter Two or elsewhere to define what the differences between Hakka and Punti were. Similarly, though the Tanka are mentioned more than once, little more is noted than that they are boat-dwellers. Nor were these three peoples the only inhabitants of the county. At least one other group — a sea-faring people known as the Hoklo 福佬 — lived around the coasts.

Of the Tanka, Qu Dajun wrote:

> The Dan 蜑 use boats as their homes 家, hence the name Danjia 蜑家 [Tanka]. To invite the attentions of matchmakers unbetrothed men place a bowl of grass on the stern of the boat, and unbetrothed girls do the same with a bowl of flowers. At the wedding the couple sing folk songs at each other, and the man takes the girl to his boat when his songs triumph over hers. Their eldest daughters are called 'fish sisters', and their youngest 'cockle sisters'. Fish are large and cockles small and hence the terms. The Dan are good swimmers. With knives and spears they will dive into the waters and fight great fish. If they see a big one in a cave they will sometimes tease it, stroking its scales and fins until it opens its mouth wide, when they impale it through both cheeks with hooks attached to long ropes and then drag it up out of the water. And sometimes scores of men will co-operate to spread a net, then some of them dive into the water and entice the fish into it, whereupon it is drawn up with the men in it as well, and it has happened that men have been eaten by the fish in the process. Sometimes a great fish will return to its cave, blocking the opening, and any men inside drown because they are unable to get

> out ..... The Dan women love eating raw fish and can all swim. In ancient times the Dan were called the Dragon people because they tattooed their faces and bodies to look like the offspring of flood dragons and they could swim 30 or 40 *li* without coming to harm ..... The women can jump and throw, fight, steer, handle fishing equipment, run and make their own living.[24]

Clearly there were differences between the Tanka and the land-dwelling Punti and Hakka, yet there is little to show that the differences were much greater than could be accounted for by the demands of a life afloat.[25]

> Admittedly, the boat people show certain peculiarities of their own in dialect as well as in manners and morals. Admittedly they tend to regard themselves as a distinct group set apart from other land-dwellers. They love to idealize themselves and say they share an ancestry of their own and belong therefore to a unique clan. But the distinguishing traits they display stem from occupational necessities. They are not necessarily racial or ethnical.[26]

The Hoklo spoke a dialect of Fujian Province — their name means 'Men from Fujian' — and did not always use the same anchorages as the Tanka, though some intermarriage between the two groups has been reported.[27] Their boats were distinguished by the eyes painted on the bows, and they had different dress and customs.[28] The gazetteer, however, does not mention their existence as a separate group, and they were presumably to be considered, like the Tanka, an aberrant group who were useful as fishermen, who caused much trouble through their mobility and rapacity at sea, but who could be brought to normal civilized behaviour if allowed to settle 'as good solid citizens' on land.[29]

It was of course the land-dwellers who most exercised the thoughts of the administration. The arrival of so many newcomers in the county after the coastal evacuation had brought with it at least one serious problem — conflict between Hakka and Punti. The major wars between the two groups had yet to come when the gazetteer was compiled in 1819,[30] but the setting up of special pass quotas for Hakka men taking the civil service examinations is an indication that this group had been discriminated against. The careful division of villages into Hakka and Punti categories is another.

The Hakka, coming in later than did most of the Punti, were generally able to gain only the less good land, and they were accordingly poorer and forced to lead a somewhat different way of life. Their women did not bind their feet and worked in the fields alongside (and sometimes instead of) the men. Certain occupations which were less desirable in Chinese society — such as tinker, blacksmith, hempweaver, building labourer, barber, and stonemason — were often carried on by Hakka men on an itinerant basis.[31] The result was that where they formed the minority of the local population the Hakka were often despised and even considered primitive and non-Chinese by their neighbours.

> There are at least five theories which attempt to explain the origin and history of the Hakka people:
> (1) The Hakkas are descendants of the Mongol garrison soldiers.
> (2) The Hakkas are aborigines from Fukien who had been assimilated by the Chinese.
> (3) The Hakkas are descendants of the half million soldiers sent by T'sin Shih Huang, many of whom intermarried with I-Kia 夷家 women.
> (4) The Hakkas are descended from the remnants of the Kingdom of Yüeh which was destroyed by Ch'u 楚 in 333 BC.
> (5) The Hakkas are descendants of Chinese coming from the Northern section of China following the Chin and T'ang dynasties.[32]

In fact there seems little reason to suppose that the Hakka are any less Chinese than the Punti. Both peoples have had a similar long-term southward migration pattern,[33] and both have undoubtedly gained an admixture of non-Chinese blood in the process. A recent study sums up the position succinctly:

> an estimated population of twenty to thirty million Hakkas spreads around at least seven provinces in China ... They are mostly farmers living in the highlands or countryside. They identify themselves as originally from the Central Plains of China — an identification of their proud ethnic origin that Hakka intellectuals sought with unusual zeal at the beginning of the modern period and which is largely supported by various historical as well as linguistic evidence. The hardships the newcomers had to endure among the southern 'natives' kept the cultural as well as linguistic unity of this group very sound, and it is fairly conspicuous even nowadays that they readily identify themselves as Hakkas regardless of their present circumstances.[34]

Yet, despite the mutually unintelligible languages, despite differences in dress, differences in degree of equality of the sexes and differences in customs, there is evidence that in Xin'an there could be close co-operation and even intermarriage between the two:

> A mixed Hakka-Punti language is still to be found in some areas of the New Territories among the older generation, known to its speakers as *wai tau wa* [圍頭話] ..... There are, as Balfour wrote before the war, 'many cases of Punti and Hakka sharing villages'. This mixed settlement is often of long standing. The good relations, or at least peaceful coexistence, that seem to have characterized it, modify

> the uniformly hostile picture of Hakka-Punti relationships in the province that may be assumed from the literature.[35]

It is possible that the administration was reflecting difficulties experienced elsewhere in Guangdong when it made such a rigorous separation between Hakka and Punti. Certainly the bulk of the gazetteer does not discriminate between different types of people. Indeed, judging by some of the items included, it appears that its compilers had a rather low opinion of the entire populace. The people spoke badly,[36] oppressed the weak,[37] gambled excessively,[38] were lawless,[39] and were more interested in quick profit than steady employment.[40] On the other hand they were 'straightforward in their dealings',[41] were handicapped by their poverty,[42] were nevertheless not without their share of worthy men and women,[43] and in their lawlessness were perhaps as much sinned against as sinning.[44]

地圖

MAPS

三角山
三門海
虎門
龍穴洲
校杯山
周家村
合水口村
邑厲壇
仙洞
歸德場
福永巡司
西鄉
黃田
固戍烟墩
新安縣
社稷壇
海光寺
馬鞍洲
桑洲山
零丁洋
大王洋
赤灣廟

Map 1

Xin'an County 1688

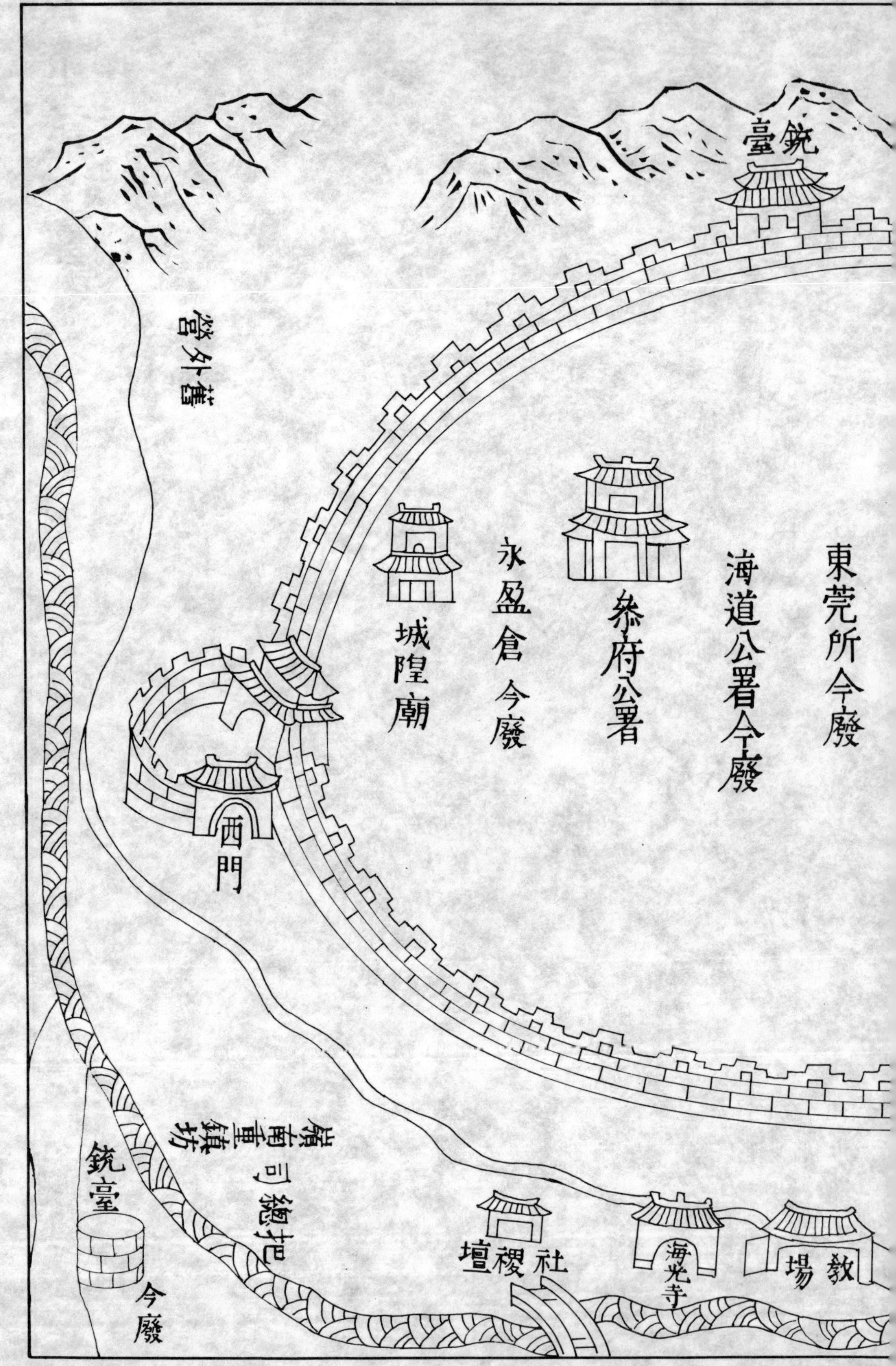

銃臺
舊外營
東莞所今廢
海道公署今廢
叅府公署
永盈倉今廢
城隍廟
西門
廣南重鎮坊
把總司
銃臺
今廢
社稷壇
海光寺
教場

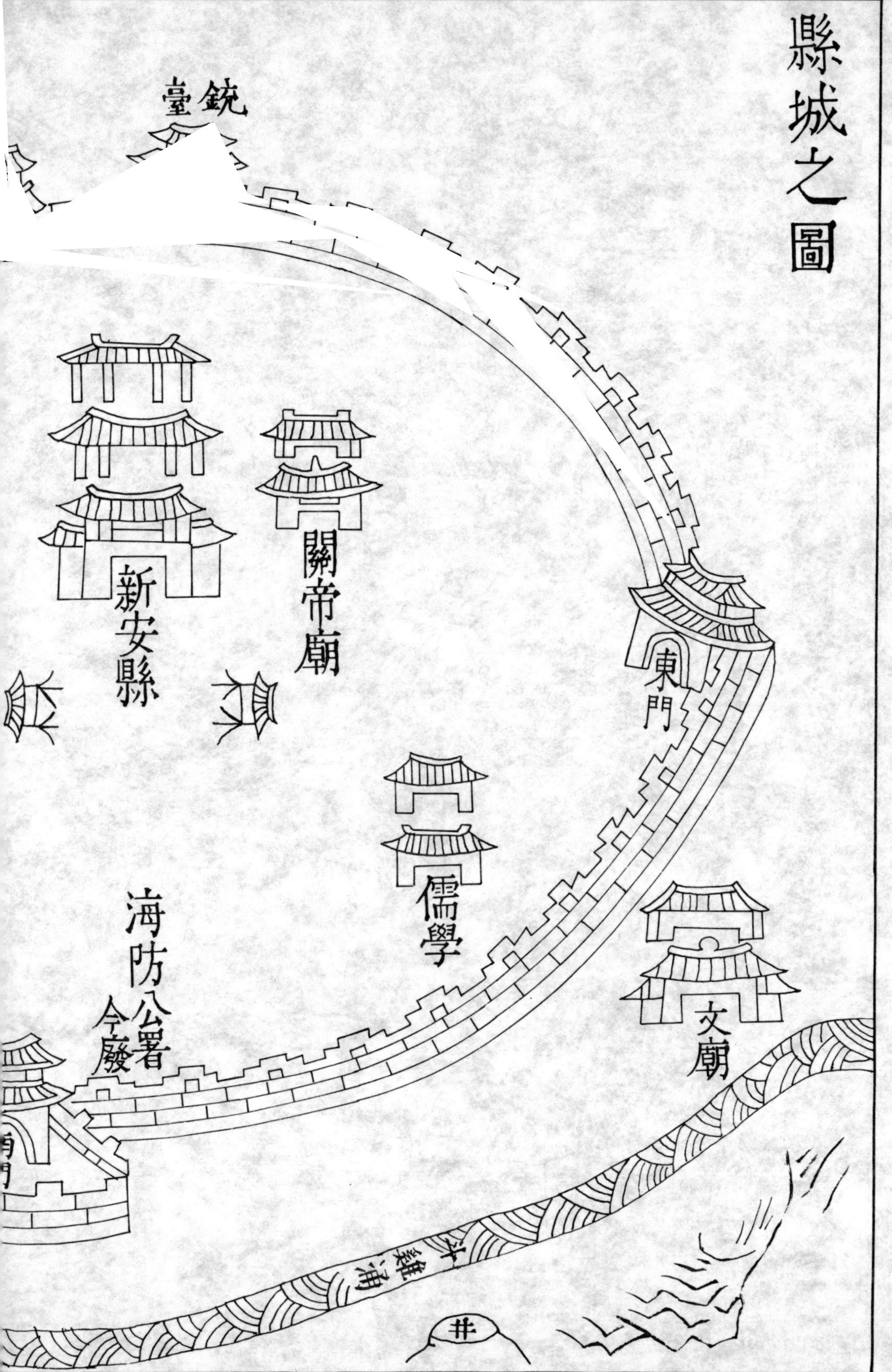

Xin'an City 1688

西北至合瀾海面八十里與東莞縣缺口司分界
莞縣缺口司分界
西至帆石海面五十里與香山縣淇澳司分界
西南至三牙牌山一百二十里與香山縣澳門廳分界
里外屬黑水大大洋
大屏帳
合水口
水貝
四都
李松蓢
羅田
燕村
塘下涌
溪頭
沙浦
碧頭
周家村
睦敦
東坑
石家村
陽台山
黃松岡
茅洲
新橋
蛋家蓢
墨頭岡
沙井
衙邊
塘下
合瀾海
固戍
福永司
三都
黃田
嶺下
白石下
西鄉
上村
二都
隔岸
留仙洞
文岡山
新安城
南頭六鋪
龍穴
帆石
南山
伶仃山
鴉仔山
聖山
龍鼓洲
三牙牌
萬山
大磨刀
小磨刀
大奚山
山

碧縣歸善與里十五百一山凹鄉西至北東
北至羊凹山八十
甲司分界
梧桐山
凹鄉西
寶山
七都
大鵬城
塩田
黄貝嶺
疊福
東至三管筆海面二百二十里與歸善縣碧甲司分界
崖紫角
下沙塘
六都
深圳
官富司
老大鵬
三管筆
雙魚各村
大埗頭
五都
錦田
大帽山
官富山
梅蔚山
洛格洲
急水門
長洲山
東南至沱濘山二百四十
沱濘
南至担竿山海面
里與歸善縣碧甲司分界

觀音閣
城隍廟
遊府署
富有倉
節孝祠
三官堂
文岡書院
今圮
社稷壇
潮音菴
海光寺
山川壇
演武亭
關帝廟
汪劉祠
南山

Map 4

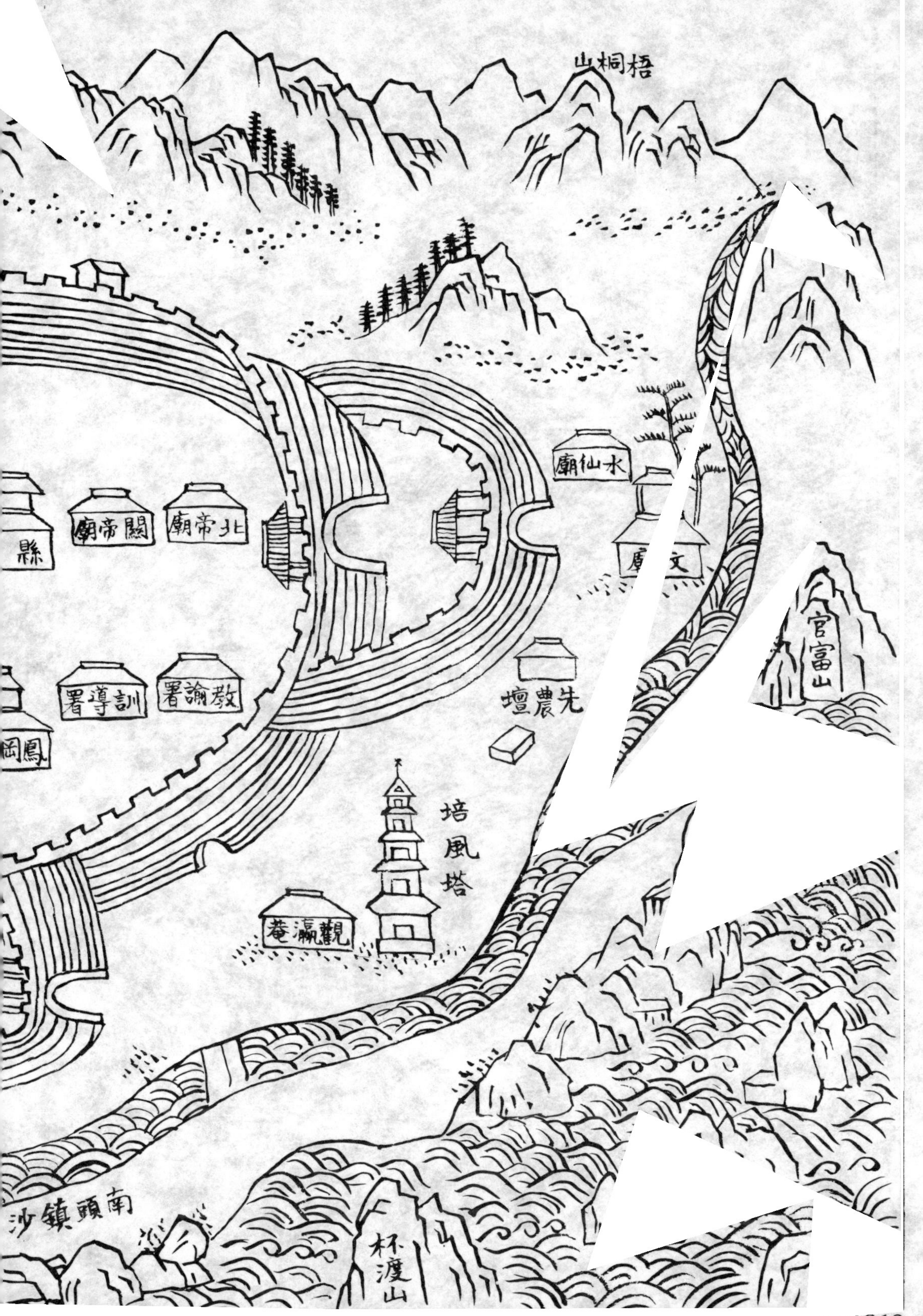

Xin an City 1819

梧桐山
九頓山
盐田汛
大梅沙
溪涌
上洞塘
疊福
橫岡
碧洲
下沙
南
九龍

Map 5

Dapeng City 1819

碧頭汛
蓮花徑
福永司署
茅洲汛
新安城
陽台山
官富司署
合瀾海
南頭炮台
南山
帆石
右炮台
屯門汛
杯渡山
左炮台
龍鼓
琵琶洲
內伶仃
哨洲
大奚山
急水門
雞翼角
萬山砲台
分流外洋
外伶仃
長洲

Xin'an County Coastal Defences 1819

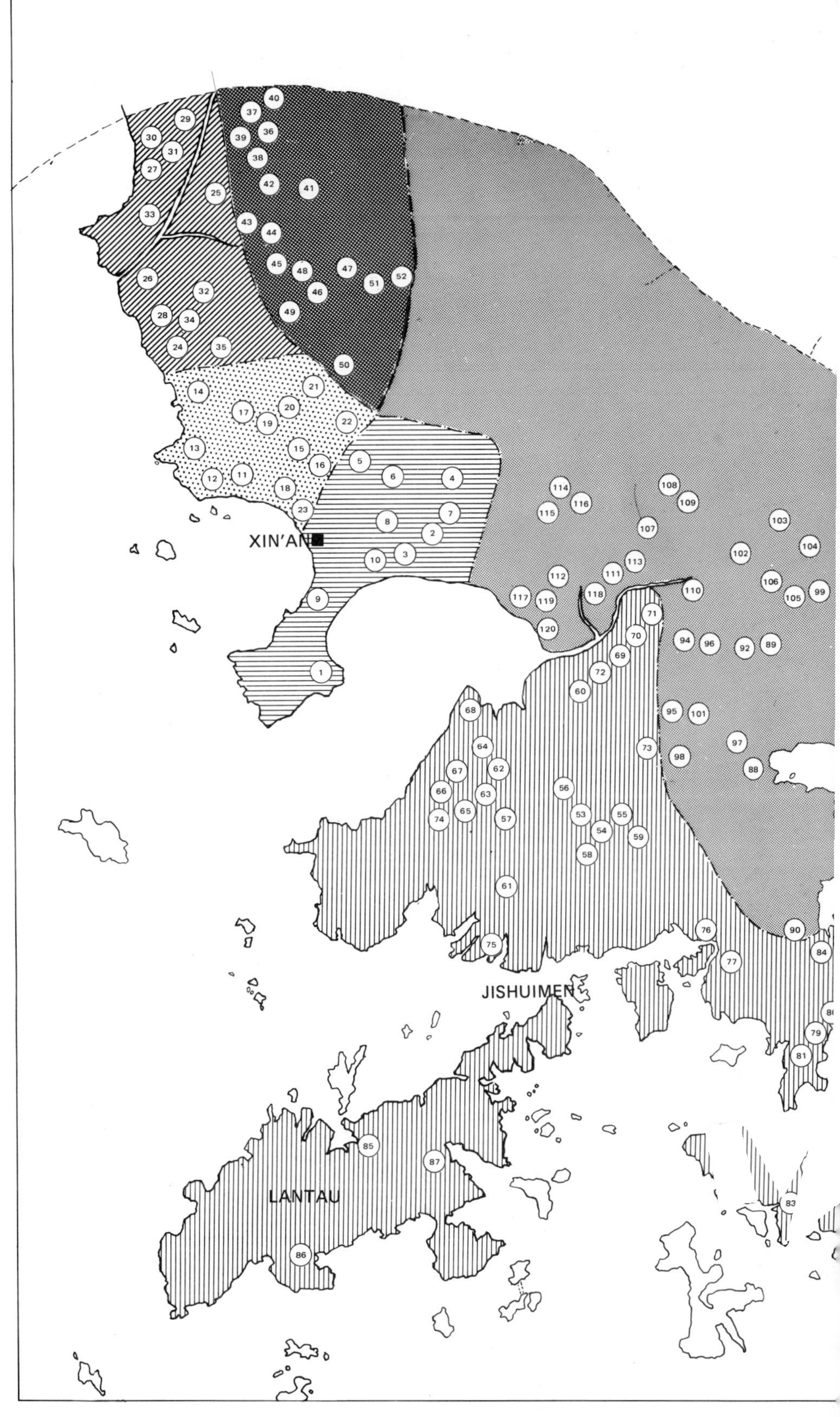
XIN'AN
JISHUIMEN
LANTAU

Map 7

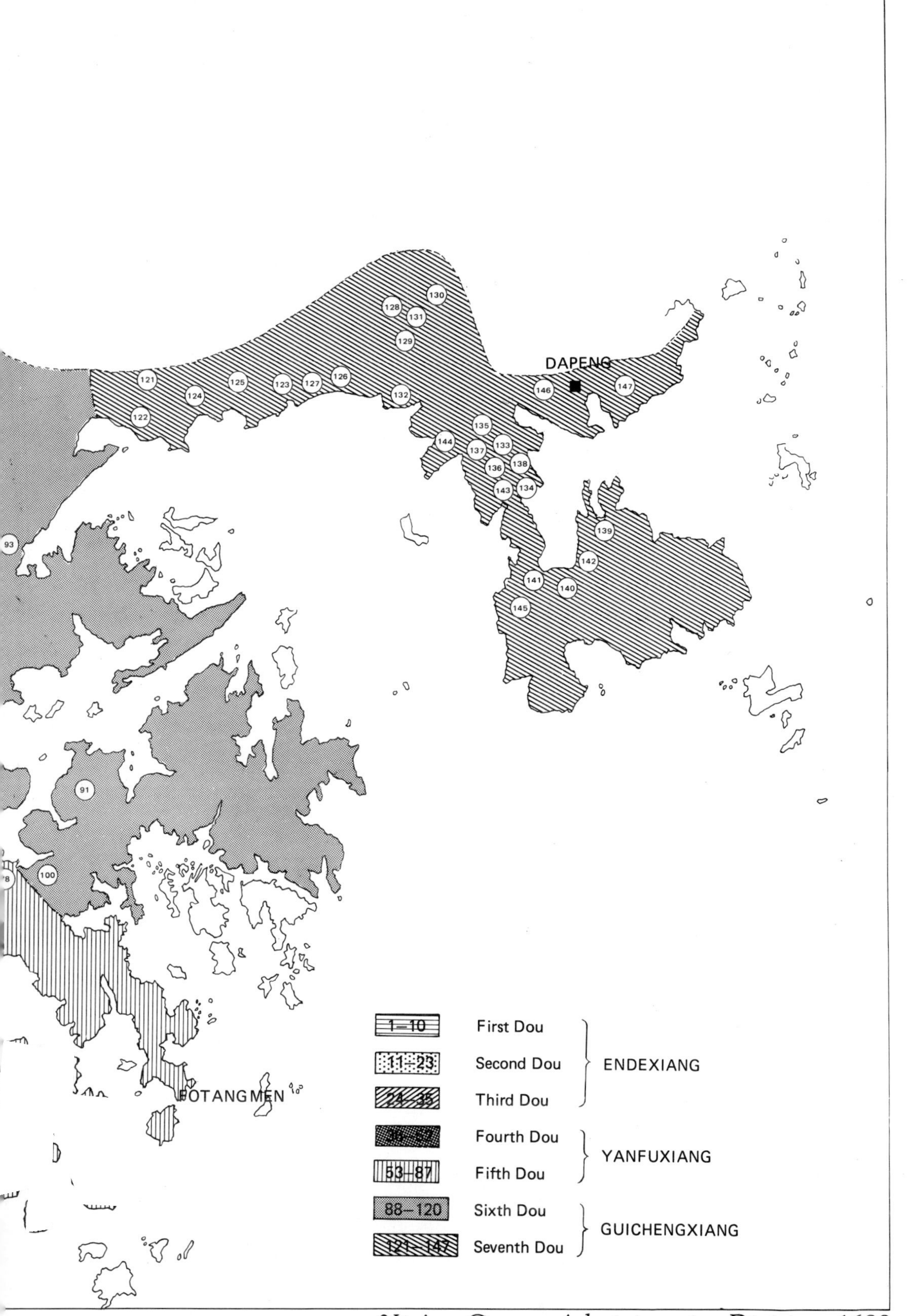

Xin'an County Administrative Divisions 1688

KEY TO MAP 7: Xin'an County Administrative Divisions 1688

The approximate locations of the one hundred and forty-seven villages which can be identified with some certainty are plotted on an outline map from the *Guangdong yudi quantu* 廣東輿地全圖 (1897) to show the boundaries of the *dou* divisions. The villages are numbered in the order in which they appear in the 1688 gazetteer. Three hundred and eighty-two other villages which could not be identified on maps have been omitted.

FIRST DOU

1. Wanxiacun 灣下村
2. Xintangcun 新塘村
3. Baishicun 白石村
4. Tanglangcun 塘莿村
5. Xinweicun 新圍村
6. Pingshancun 平山村
7. Longjingcun 龍井村
8. Zhugangtou 珠岡頭
9. Nantoucun 南頭村
10. Dayongcun 大涌村

SECOND DOU

11. Xixiangcun 西鄉村
12. Aowancun 鰲灣村
13. Guxucun 固戍村
14. Huangtiancun 黃田村
15. Zhuangbiancun 庄邊村
16. Puxincun 莆心村
17. Liutangcun 流塘村
18. Shangcun 上村
19. Tiegangcun 鐵岡村
20. Baishacun 白沙村
21. Tangtoucun 塘頭村
22. Niushengcun 牛繩村
23. Ge'an 隔岸

THIRD DOU

24. Fuyongcun 福永村
25. Maozhouxu 茅洲墟
26. Bitoucun 碧頭村
27. Tangxiacun 塘下村
28. Qiaotoucun 橋頭村
29. Liugangcun 流岡村
30. Tantoucun 潭頭村
31. Xinqiaocun 新橋村
32. Lingxiacun 嶺下村
33. Dengjialang 鄧家莿
34. Baishixia 白石下
35. Huangmapu 黃蔴莆

FOURTH DOU

36. Shuibeicun 水貝村
37. Heguling 禾穀嶺
38. Heshuikou 合水口
39. Zhoujiacun 周家村
40. Mashantou 馬山頭
41. Sumugang 粟木岡
42. Tangjiacun 唐家村
43. Tianliaoxia 田寮下
44. Yulecun 玉勒村
45. Jingbeicun 逕背村
46. Luozucun 羅租村
47. Guantiancun 官田村
48. Wushiyan 烏石巖
49. Wangjiazhuang 王家庄
50. Yingrenshi 應人石
51. Bainikeng 白坭坑
52. Tangkengcun 棠坑村

FIFTH DOU

53. Jintiancun 錦田村
54. Yuangangcun 圓岡村
55. Shangcuncun 上村村
56. Shapuwei 沙莆圍
57. Yuanlang 圓莿
58. Changpuwei 長莆圍
59. Shigangwei 石岡圍
60. Zhuyuanwei 竹園圍
61. Baishawei 白沙圍
62. Shuijiaowei 水蕉圍
63. Hengzhoucun 橫州村
64. Dajingcun 大井村
65. Pingshancun 屏山村

66. Shibucun 石步村
67. Xiacuncun 厦村村
68. Wangjingcun 輞井村
69. Xintiancun 新田村
70. Zhoutoucun 洲頭村
71. Lemazhou 勒馬州
72. Mibucun 米步村
73. Jiaojingcun 蕉逕村
74. Xishancun 西山村
75. Saoguanyu 掃管鬱
76. Qianwancun 淺灣村
77. Kuiyongcun 葵涌村
78. Shatiancun 沙田村
79. Guanfucun 官富村
80. Yaqiancun 衙前村
81. Jiulongcun 九龍村
82. Huangniyong 黄坭涌
83. Xianggangcun 香港村
84. Liyuancun 瀝源村
85. Dongxiyong 東西涌
86. Shibicun 石壁村
87. Meiwocun 梅窩村

SIXTH DOU

88. Dabutou 大步頭
89. Longyuetou 龍躍頭
90. Jingkoucun 逕口村
91. Zhangmutou 樟木頭
92. Longtangcun 龍塘村
93. Maqiaoling 蔴雀嶺
94. Heshangxiang 河尚鄉
95. Binggangcun 丙岡村
96. Shangshuicun 上水村
97. Taikengcun 泰坑村
98. Lincuncun 林村村
99. Wanwubian 萬屋邊
100. Xiaoliyuan 小瀝源
101. Fenbiling 粉壁嶺
102. Huangbeiling 黄貝嶺
103. Henggangcun 横岡村
104. Lianmakeng 蓮蔴坑
105. Danzhukeng 丹竹坑
106. Shanjiyu 山鷄鬱
107. Sungangcun 笋岡村
108. Xinwubian 新屋邊
109. Tianxincun 田心村
110. Luohucun 羅湖村
111. Chiweicun 赤尾村
112. Gangxiacun 岡下村
113. Shangbucun 上步村
114. Shangmeilin 上梅林
115. Xiameilin 下梅林
116. Lingbeicun 嶺貝村
117. Shatouxu 沙頭墟
118. Getiancun 隔田村
119. Shaweicun 沙尾村
120. Xinzaocun 新竈村

SEVENTH DOU

121. Kucaotong 苦草峒
122. Shagangxu 沙岡墟
123. Qiyongcun 溪涌村
124. Dameisha 大梅沙
125. Xiaomeisha 小梅沙
126. Shangdong 上洞
127. Xiadong 下洞
128. Kuiyongcun 葵涌村
129. Aotoucun 凹頭村
130. Disanqi 第三溪
131. Gaozhentou 高圳頭
132. Guanhucun 關湖村
133. Shuibeicun 水貝村
134. Longqicun 龍岐村
135. Huangmutong 黄母峒
136. Xinqiaocun 新橋村
137. Shiqiaotou 石橋頭
138. Shapucun 沙莆村
139. Huoduicun 火堆村
140. Henggangcun 横岡村
141. Dalingxia 大嶺下
142. Hengkengcun 横坑村
143. Shijiaotou 石角頭
144. Diefucun 疊福村
145. Bantianyun 半天雲
146. Wuyongcun 烏涌村
147. Dakengcun 大坑村

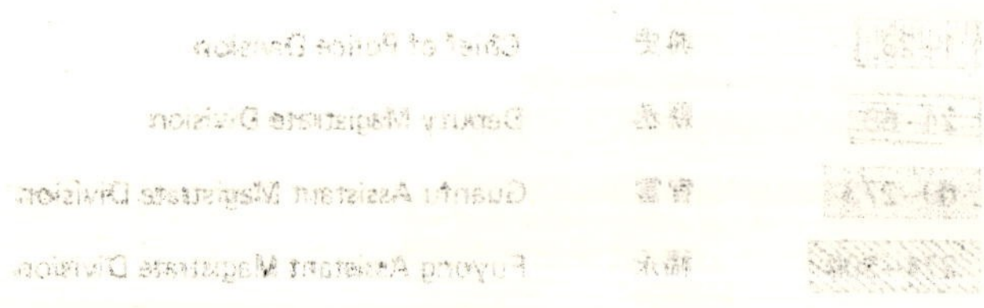

KEY TO MAP 8: Xin'an County Administrative Divisions 1819

Three hundred and nine villages listed in the 1819 gazetteer have been identified on maps and their approximate locations plotted on the same outline as Map 7 to show the four administrative divisions then in force. As with Map 7 the villages are numbered in the order in which they appear in the gazetteer. A further five hundred and forty-eight villages are listed but cannot be identified with certainty.

CHIEF OF POLICE DIVISION

1. Nantou 南頭
2. Shiqiaotou 石橋頭
3. Guankou 關口
4. Xiangnancun 向南村
5. Diyijia 第一甲
6. Duntoucun 墩頭村
7. Xixiang 西鄉
8. Baishicun 白石村
9. Xintangcun 莘塘村
10. Anqiancun 庵前村
11. Xinweicun 新圍村
12. Tanglangcun 塘蓢村
13. Tiegangcun 鐵岡村
14. Zhu'aocun 猪凹村
15. Pingshancun 平山村
16. Zhugangtou 珠岡頭
17. Xilicun 西瀝村
18. Aowancun 鰲灣村
19. Longjingcun 龍井村
20. Wanxiacun 灣下村
21. Puxincun 莆心村
22. Changlingpi 長嶺皮
23. Lingdingcun 伶仃村

DEPUTY MAGISTRATE DIVISION

24. Shuibeicun 水貝村
25. Tianxinwei 田心圍
26. Dakengcun 大坑村
27. Dongcun 東村
28. Bantianyun 半天雲
29. Xigongwei 西貢圍
30. Nanshewei 南社圍
31. Shagangwei 沙岡圍
32. Dalingxia 大嶺下
33. Pingshanzi 坪山仔
34. Shuitoucun 水頭村
35. Puweicun 埔尾村
36. Wangmuxu 王母墟
37. Yamujiao 鴨母脚
38. Gaozhentou 高圳頭
39. Dameisha 大梅沙
40. Xiaomeisha 小梅沙
41. Qiyongcun 溪涌村
42. Shangdong 上洞
43. Xiadong 下洞
44. Pingzhoucun 平洲村
45. Shayuyong 沙魚涌
46. Guanhucun 關湖村
47. Niuchunling 牛唇嶺
48. Shiqiaotou 石橋頭
49. Kewuwei 柯屋圍
50. Egongcun 鵝公村
51. Shuitousha 水頭沙
52. Youcaopeng 油草棚
53. Huangqi Tang 黄旗塘
54. Qisha 岐沙
55. Hengkeng 横坑
56. Shijiaotou 石角頭
57. Dadui 大碓
58. Longqicun 龍岐村
59. Xiasha 下沙
60. Diefu 疊福
61. Shuitou 水頭
62. Kuiyongxu 葵涌墟
63. Tuyang 土洋
64. Disanqi 第三溪
65. Jingxin 逕心
66. Fengshutou 楓樹頭
67. Baishigang 白石岡
68. Aotou 凹頭

GUANFU ASSISTANT MAGISTRATE DIVISION

69. Jintiancun 錦田村
70. Pingshancun 屏山村
71. Xiachuancun 厦川村
72. Xinweicun 新圍村
73. Tunmencun 屯門村
74. Xishancun 西山村
75. Wangzhencun 輞川村
76. Shigangwei 石岡圍
77. Shangcuncun 上村村
78. Shapuwei 沙莆圍
79. Zhuyuanwei 竹園圍
80. Yuanlang 元蓢
81. Baishacun 白沙村
82. Tianxinwei 田心圍
83. Shibu 石步
84. Zhangwucun 張屋村
85. Dajingcun 大井村
86. Hengzhoucun 横洲村
87. Putangxia 莆塘下
88. Xiaokengcun 小坑村
89. Meiwocun 梅窩村
90. Shibicun 石壁村
91. Shalowan 沙螺灣
92. Tangfucun 塘福村
93. Er'aocun 二奧村
94. Yougulang 由古蓢
95. Pingzhouwan 平洲灣
96. Longyuetou 龍躍頭
97. Heshangxiang 河上鄉
98. Jinqiancun 金錢村
99. Yangangcun 燕岡村
100. Binggangcun 丙岡村
101. Shangshuicun 上水村
102. Pushangcun 莆上村
103. Fenbiling 粉壁嶺
104. Songbolang 松柏蓢
105. Gudongcun 古洞村
106. Shihuxu 石湖墟
107. Zhoutoucun 洲頭村
108. Xintiancun 新田村
109. Mibucun 米步村
110. Jundicun 軍地村
111. Danzhukeng 丹竹坑
112. Taihengcun 泰亨村
113. Dabutou 大步頭
114. Dabuxu 大步墟
115. Dawo 大窩
116. Nankengcun 南坑村
117. Fengyuancun 豐園村
118. Zhongwucun 鍾屋村
119. Tangmiancun 塘面村
120. Wuqisha 烏溪沙
121. Zhangmutou 樟木頭
122. Xi'aocun 西澳村
123. Jingtou 井頭
124. Dadongcun 大洞村
125. Xijingcun 西逕村
126. Rongshu'ao 榕樹澳
127. Magulan 馬牯纜
128. Shajiaowei 沙角尾
129. Beigangcun 北港村
130. Houyongcun 蠔涌村
131. Beitancun 北潭村
132. Chijingcun 赤逕村
133. Ma'an Shan 馬鞍山
134. Tianxincun 田心村
135. Jingkoucun 逕口村
136. Getiancun 隔田村
137. Xiaoliyuan 小瀝源
138. Jiulongzhai 九龍寨
139. Yaqiancun 衙前村
140. Changshawan 長沙灣
141. Jianshatou 尖沙頭
142. Wangjiaocun 芒角村
143. Tuguawan 土瓜灣
144. Shenshuipu 深水莆
145. Huangniyong 黃泥涌
146. Xianggangcun 香港村
147. Baoliaocun 薄寮村
148. Baofulin 薄鳧林
149. Xiangxicun 向西村
150. Hubeicun 湖貝村
151. Shuibeicun 水貝村
152. Huangbeiling 黃貝嶺
153. Shangbucun 上步村

154. Lohucun 羅湖村
155. Chiweicun 赤尾村
156. Liwucun 李屋村
157. Daputian 大莆田
158. Shanjiyu 山鷄鬱
159. Lofangcun 羅坊村
160. Aoxiacun 凹下村
161. Henggangxia 横岡下
162. Dajingcun 大逕村
163. Sungangcun 筍岡村
164. Shangmeilin 上梅林
165. Xiameilin 下梅林
166. Shixia 石下
167. Shazuicun 沙嘴村
168. Shaweicun 沙尾村
169. Xihecun 西河村
170. Shatou 沙頭
171. Xinzaocun 新灶村
172. Futiancun 福田村
173. Gangxiacun 岡下村
174. Lingbeicun 嶺貝村
175. Baishilong 白石龍
176. Zhucuncun 竹村村
177. Qinghucun 清湖村
178. Shangfen 上芬
179. Huangshakeng 黄沙坑
180. Kucaodong 苦草洞
181. Yantian 鹽田
182. Puge 莆隔
183. Caopuzi 草莆仔
184. Dawangzi 大輞仔
185. Zhangshupu 樟樹莆
186. Lilang 李蓢
187. Lianmakeng 蓮麻坑
188. Gankeng 柑坑
189. Dafen 大芬
190. Xintianzi 新田子
191. Niweizi 泥圍子
192. Danzhutou 丹竹頭
193. Mumianwan 木棉灣
194. Chikantou 企墈頭
195. Shangxiaping 上下坪
196. Xiangyuan 香園
197. Liantang 蓮塘
198. Hekeng 禾坑
199. Pingyang 平洋
200. Wanwubian 萬屋邊
201. Majiaoling 麻雀嶺
202. Nanyongwei 南涌圍
203. Qimuqiao 七木橋
204. Lujing 鹿頸
205. Wujiaotian 烏蛟田
206. Lizhiwo 荔枝窩
207. Gubu 谷埠
208. Fengkeng 風坑
209. Rongshu'ao 榕樹凹
210. Xincun 新村
211. Danshuikeng 担水坑
212. Shajingtou 沙井頭
213. Shanzui 山嘴
214. Jingkou 逕口
215. Aotou 凹頭
216. Anjing 暗逕
217. Jinzhucun 金竹村
218. Yuanduntou 園墪頭
219. Aobeizi 凹背子
220. Longyanyuan 龍眼園
221. Tunwei 屯圍
222. Honggang 紅崗
223. Xiaopu 小莆
224. Shagangxu 沙岡墟
225. Wanyao 碗窰
226. Shalodong 沙螺洞
227. Weixia 圍下
228. Pingshanzi 坪山仔
229. Puxinpai 莆心排
230. Huangyutan 黄魚灘
231. Dongzi 洞子
232. She Shan 社山
233. Bo'ao Shi 栢鰲石
234. Wutongzhai 梧桐寨
235. Zhaiji 寨乪
236. Dawangche 大芒輋
237. Da'ang 大菴
238. Jiaojing 蕉逕
239. Shangxiache 上下輋

240. Hengtai Shan 橫台山
241. Ma'angang 馬鞍岡
242. Changpu 長莆
243. Dalan 大欖
244. Saoguanyu 掃管鬱
245. Dawo 大窩
246. Chengmen 城門
247. Chuanlong 穿龍
248. Qianwan 淺灣
249. Kuiyongzi 葵涌子
250. Qingyi 青衣
251. Liantangwei 蓮塘尾
252. Menggongwu 孟公屋
253. Binlangwan 檳榔灣
254. Yuhewan 芋合灣
255. Lanniwan 爛坭灣
256. Lizhizhuang 荔枝庄
257. Shatian 沙田
258. Xuezhujing 雪竹逕
259. Yuanfen 緣分
260. Gangtouzi 岡頭子
261. Yangwei 羊尾
262. Xiangjiaotang 象角塘
263. Pantianzi 泮田子
264. Chilingtou 赤嶺頭
265. Zaohekeng 早禾坑
266. Lushengtang 盧盛塘
267. Langkou 蓢口
268. Shi'ao 石凹
269. Jueling 蕨嶺
270. Xikeng 西坑
271. Henglang 橫蓢
272. Laiwu Shan 賴屋山
273. Ji'ao 吉澳

FUYONG ASSISTANT MAGISTRATE DIVISION

274. Shuibeicun 水貝村
275. Heshuikou 合水口
276. Mashantou 馬山頭
277. Tianliaoxia 田寮下
278. Bitoucun 碧頭村
279. Maozhou Shan 茅洲山
280. Tantoucun 潭頭村
281. Lougangcun 樓岡村
282. Huangsonggang 黃松岡
283. Tangxiayong 塘下涌
284. Tangjiacun 唐家村
285. Longwancun 龍灣村
286. Hequling 禾曲嶺
287. Huangjiazhuang 黃家庄
288. Langxincun 蓢心村
289. Zhenlongcun 鎮龍村
290. Shajingcun 沙井村
291. Dawang Shan 大王山
292. Lingxiacun 嶺下村
293. Baishicun 白石村
294. Guxucun 固戍村
295. Dengjialang 鄧家蓢
296. Shatoucun 沙頭村
297. Qiaotoucun 橋頭村
298. Gangguling 更鼓嶺
299. Guantian 官田
300. Mapucun 蔴莆村
301. Jingbeicun 逕貝村
302. Nigang 坭岡
303. Lozucun 羅祖村
304. Tangkengwei 塘坑圍
305. Apoji 亞婆髻
306. Huangmapu 黃蔴莆
307. Lizhutang 蓠竹塘
308. Zheyuanpu 蔗園莆
309. Yingrenshi 應人石

3. ECONOMY

The economy of Xin'an was different from the simple agricultural economy of most of the other regions of the Chinese Empire. Farming, it is true, played the leading role in the county's economic life, and land-tax was the main source of official revenue as it was elsewhere; but the geographical conditions of Xin'an made possible the development of two other industries which were tapped by the government for revenue — fishing and salt production.

The gazetteer does not set aside a chapter exclusively for discussion of the occupations of the people. In Chapter Three a list of agricultural products is given, as well as a list of the fishes which can be found in the county's waters; in Chapter Eight are details of how farmers, fishermen and salt-makers were taxed by the government; the three major occupations are also mentioned here and there in the edicts reproduced in the Premier Chapter and in the memorials and proposals written by Xin'an officials which are quoted in Chapter Twenty-two. But these major industries are discussed from the point of view of the administrators rather than of those who actually worked in them. Only in passing does the human element intrude — such as in the 'Natural Disasters' section of Chapter Thirteen. The resulting picture of the economy is neither broad nor clear.

Agriculture

Agriculture, and in particular the growing of grain, was a major concern of administration and people alike. The soils of Xin'an were capable of producing high quality rice, and with two crops per year (even three in a few specially favoured locations such as the Lincun 林村 valley) and a possible catch crop of vegetables in the dry winter months the county could be self-sufficient in food.

> The rice from Shatin Valley was reputed to be the finest in China, and was sent as part of the annual tribute to the Emperor in Peiping.[1]

Early rice was planted in March and harvested in July, and the late crop period was July to November. A small amount of hill paddy was grown as an early crop; and in soils with a high salt content, such as those of the Deep Bay marsh area, a brackish-water paddy crop was grown in the late summer.[2] The gazetteer lists by name five varieties of early first crop rice, three of late first crop, four of first crop 'dry' 赤 rice and two of first crop glutinous rice. For the second crop it gives two early, four late, four glutinous, and one brackish variety.[3]

As well as rice other grains could be grown, and the gazetteer notes three kinds of millet and three of wheat. The 'Grains' section also includes a list of eight different pulses, three types of taro, three kinds of sesame and eight varieties of yam 薯 :

> There are several types of yam grown in the county: there is the sweet yam, the mountain yam, the sweet potato, the linen yam, the hairy yam, the red yam, the white yam and the greater yam. Of these the sweet potato is used by the local people as a substitute for rice. It is an extremely nutritious characteristic food of the area.[4]

The sweet potato 番薯 was imported to China in the late sixteenth century. High-yielding, nutritious, drought resistant and able to flourish in poor soils so that it did not compete with other crops, it soon became established:

> In the southeastern coastal provinces, which were always deficient in rice and where the people were long accustomed to Chinese yams and taros as secondary food, the sweet potato suited the dietary habit of the maritimers and was promptly welcomed. It soon became the poor man's staple....Since China's population was increasing rapidly after 1700, a series of imperial edicts and provincial circulars exhorted the northern peasants to grow sweet potatoes on a large scale, in order to stave off famine.[5]

Yet an edict in 1727 addressed to the people of Fujian and Guangdong provinces does not refer to sweet potatoes, urging that more rice should be grown and less attention be paid to cash crops.[6]

The *longan* 龍眼 or 'dragon's eye' is one of the cash crops mentioned in the edict, but the entry under *longan* in the 'Fruits' section says nothing of its being grown commercially:

> The *longan* or *longmu* 龍目 is a greenish-brown fruit, round like a ball, with a soft woody kernel. The flesh is white and juicy and sweet as honey. They grow in clusters like grapes, and ripen just as the litchi season finishes. Hence they are also known as 'litchi slaves' because they are said to 'follow along behind them'.[7]

Other fruits mentioned are the sand-pear, the orange, the pomelo, the tangerine ('good for sobering up'), the carambola, the banana, the lemon (entered under the name 'mother's comfort' 宜母果 because 'eating it calms pregnant women who feel uneasy'), the *wongpe* 黃皮 ('offsets the effects of over-eating litchis'), the *miwang* 蜜望 (which can 'quell sea-sickness'), the peach, the water-melon, the pineapple, the peanut, two kinds of sugar-cane, and the *youganzi* 油柑子 (guava?). None of these entries indicates commercial exploitation.

The 'Vegetables' section is less detailed, merely listing seven spring vegetables, six summer and five autumn/winter ones, plus the onion 'which can be had at all seasons'. Included also are seaweeds: kelp 'which can cure lumps in the throat', horsetail, gum-weed 'much prized by craftsmen for making glue', and laver 'highly valued as a food and sold to a wide market'.[8] This last is one of the very few references found in the entire chapter to the selling of produce.

The 'Trees' section contains only three entries. The banyan takes pride of place and its ability to survive in an environment where wood has long been at a premium is explained:

> Its wood is gnarled and so cannot be used as timber, it will not flame and so cannot be used for firewood. Its very lack of useful properties ensures its invulnerability and survival, and its shade covers ten *mu* 畝 .[9]

The cottonwood tree, producing floss for quilting, and the incense tree are the other two listed. The latter is said to flourish best at Shatian, on Lantau and in the Fuyong area, but there is no mention of the incense trade, which by this time must have been dead.

As is consistent with normal Chinese categorization, 'bamboos' are listed separately from 'trees'. Eleven types are named and variously designated useful in house-building, rope-making, raft-building, etc. 'Rattans' list six varieties, one poisonous and one useful in snake-catching. Several types of 'teas' are given and seven different 'herbs' and their principal properties.

Without question rice was the most important of all the crops grown in the county. An adequate water supply was vital for its success, but the eroded hillsides and broken nature of the landscape meant quick runoff of rain-water and hardly any reliable constant flowing streams. Major irrigation schemes were also inhibited by the landscape, and it seems that only in the larger plains, where strong lineages controlled their territories, were serious efforts made to improve the situation. Chapter Four lists sixteen reservoirs 陂 for the whole county, and most of them can only have been of minor importance, serving at best one village's lands:

> *Shatang Reservoir* lies behind Shangshui village. Its water supply comes more than 10 *li* from Shuimen Hill and is dammed to provide irrigation for the fields. *Shi*

> *Reservoir* is on the right-hand side of Shangshui village, taking its water from Shatang Reservoir and damming it to provide irrigation for the fields.[10]

Both reservoirs still exist. They are each no larger than 25 metres square and if they are typical of the other fourteen it is clear that the effectiveness of the irrigation schemes must have been very limited.

Disaster and relief

With such minimal control over water, both flood and drought were constant menaces. The 'Natural Disasters' section of Chapter Thirteen has some large gaps in its chronological coverage, but even so presents a dismal picture of the frequency with which excess or shortage of water brought misery to the population. In 1648 it claims that more than half the population died and people resorted to cannibalism, while in 1686 Xin'an City itself was flooded to a depth of ten feet and many people and animals were drowned. Even when the year as a whole was not too dry or too wet, one savage typhoon could bring large-scale death and destruction in just a few hours, as happened, for example, on 21 March 1671.[11]

The authorities had few answers. At the best of times they were faced with an area where basic foodstuffs were in shortage. They tried to get the people to grow more grain, and they encouraged the import of grain from overseas by remitting taxes,[12] but roads and communications were extremely poor, and they had neither the resources nor the manpower to deal with emergencies.

The front line of defence was the granary system headed by the Ever Normal Granary 常平倉 :

> [Ever Normal Granaries] were first established in 1655 by the imperial government....The grain, which might be rice, wheat, sorghum or other foodstuff, was procured by purchase with government funds as well as by contributions from all who cared to make them....The grain reserve was lent to needy peasants or sold at 'normal' (below current market) prices, as the situation required.[13]

Other granaries were supplied, maintained and run by local people as charities to supplement the official institutions. Xin'an was provided with a total of seven granaries in 1819,[14] but it is doubtful whether they were effective in alleviating hardship. In 1640, even before the system was operative, the county magistrate Zhou Xiyao was already petitioning to have the stores of grain kept low on the grounds that the county could not afford more.[15] Furthermore, abuses in the storing, allocation and repayment of the grain meant that the capacity for emergency relief was often severely compromised. The gazetteer includes an edict of 1738 which attempts to scotch one of these abuses,[16] and Krone, writing in 1858, points out that despite the gazetteer's insistence that the two major granaries at Xin'an and Dapeng contained 20,660 piculs[17] and 1,700 piculs respectively:

> even this benevolent institution is made, by the avarice of the mandarins, more a burden to the people than a means of relieving their necessities. The small quantity which is stored up is generally consumed by vermin, and nothing is left for the indigent in times of scarcity.[18]

Remission of taxes was another means of helping a stricken population:

> Whenever there was a flood or drought, it was the magistrate's duty to make a preliminary investigation and report his findings to his superior at once....The preliminary investigation was followed by a second investigation by commissioners assigned by the magistrate's superior officials, in which the magistrate also assisted. Within forty days of the second investigation, the magistrate was to submit a report on the seriousness of the calamity....The percentage of tax reduction varied according to the degree of crop damage. As a rule, the collection of tax (minus the reduction agreed upon) was postponed for one to three years after the calamity.[19]

Taxation

For purposes of taxation, land in the county was divided into three categories, superior, medium and inferior, according to the quality of the soil. Superior land was taxed at 0.0302 *dan* of grain per *mu*, medium at 0.0208 *dan* and inferior at 0.0126 *dan*. These were the rates for land owned by commoners 民竈米. The rates for land which belonged to the government 官米 were much lower at 0.0041, 0.0038 and 0.0036 *dan* respectively.[20] This was to compensate for the higher percentage of grain income which tenants of government land paid as rent.[21] The taxes were calculated in grain but could be paid in silver, conversion rates differing according to the type of land.[22] On the creation of the county in 1573 the registered land totalled some 291,147 *mu*, that is, approximately 48,000 acres. This had risen to 406,042 *mu* (66,900 acres) by 1642 when the last assessment under the Ming dynasty was made, but the figure in use in the Qing was 403,956 *mu* (66,500 acres), a small decrease. The gazetteer mentions the discrepancy but is unable to account for it 'because none of the provincial or prefectural records furnishes any relevant information'.[23] It seems likely that the coastal evacuation of 1662-69 had resulted in the abandonment of previously registered land.

The total area of taxable land varied from time to time. All land newly brought under cultivation was supposed to be reported to the yamen, and assessments made accordingly. The normal rule governing the opening of waste-land was that the owner was exempt from tax for the first six years of cultivation in the case of paddy fields and for the first ten years in the case of terraced fields.[24] Thus 21 *mu* of waste-land was registered in 1726 and became liable for grain tax in 1736, 5,655 *mu* were registered in 1729, 151 *mu* in 1752, 12,085 *mu* between 1757 and 1761 and 599 *mu* between 1772 and 1782.[25] These figures indicate a gradual increase of arable land in the county during the eighteenth century, and this was accompanied by a rise in population.[26]

Land could also be relieved of tax liability. For example, in 1657 a total area of 17,488 *mu* was exempted from taxation in consideration of special difficulties; in 1741, 1,238 *mu* were exempted, and in 1746 an area of 55 *mu* was struck out of the tax register altogether as being incapable of producing anything.

In theory the land-tax was fixed as the sum of the land area multiplied by the tax rate. In practice it varied from year to year because it was customary for the local authorities to impose additional charges for collection. At times the central government also imposed extra charges, although this practice did not assume any serious proportions until the middle of the nineteenth century. The actual tax paid could be several times greater than the stated quota.[27] The total realized from land and miscellaneous taxes such as property deeds tax, meltage surcharges, transport fees, and surcharges for supplementary salaries for officials is stated to be just over 13,329 taels for the whole of Xin'an, this figure presumably applying at the time of the gazetteer's publication.[28]

Another source of revenue was that from the *guandi* 官地 , land owned by the state itself. Such land was rented to individual tenants, but the income accruing from it was usually spent on social services such as education, official ceremonies at the temples, and rural banquets. In the gazetteer the locations and acreages of the various areas of *guandi* together with the names of the tenants and the rentals paid are all recorded in detail, though the total area falls short of 600 *mu*. Much of the income derived from it went into the financing of public education.[29] Similarly there was the 'military farmland' 屯田 , land originally set aside for the use and upkeep of the four military garrisons, two first-class (*wei* 衞) and two second-class (*suo* 所):

> At the beginning of the Ming dynasty three-tenths of the troops were on garrison duty, while the rest lived on the farm settlements. The garrison troops were given rations, but those on the farms received none.[30]

The *wei* and *suo* were abolished in 1725 and the land came under the control of the county administration which rented it out or sold it. There was over 9,226 *mu* of land in the two *suo*, but no information is given for the *wei* other than that the land was 'in remote areas' 僻遠 .[31]

The acreage of land officially registered works out at approximately 100 square miles, that is at between a fifth and a sixth of the county's geographical area. Without question much useful occupied land remained off the registers for, were it not so, the large increases in population could not have gone on being supported by an almost constant cultivated area:

> It is clear that this highly improbable proportion between population and official land figures cannot be a reflection of the historical relation between population and land.... The traditional land returns were, in the last analysis, numbers of units in land-tax payment. They were returns of fiscal rather than actual acreage under cultivation, consequently, they were invariably too low.[32]

On the whole the land-tax burden was light. In the early Qing period land-tax and poll-tax on male adults (ding 丁) were separately assessed, but then:

> In 1713 came the highly praised decree of 永不加賦 [never raise taxes]. This decree provided that the amount of the 丁 tax in 1711 be considered the permanent quota and that the increased number of male adults afterwards would no longer be liable to the tax. But officials throughout the empire interpreted the phrase 永不加賦 literally and applied it to the landtax, especially after the merger of the 丁 tax into the landtax in the second quarter of the eighteenth century. Naturally, no increase in the landtax implied no increase in registered acreage.
>
> In the middle of the eighteenth century the government moved further along this direction by decreeing that odd pieces of newly reclaimed land in the provinces were permanently exempted from taxation (that is, exempted from registration).[33]

One recent calculation suggests that in Xin'an in the nineteenth century 'taxes consistently consumed no more than 2 per cent of the rent-value'.[34] The local situation was a complex one in that there was at work a system of tax-farming 包攬 by which major landholders, such as the Deng lineage of Jintian, not only collected rents on their own behalf but also taxes on the government's, and the true tax position is therefore hard to assess.[35] But it seems that the known reluctance of the 'tax-lords' to relinquish this function at the time of the lease of the New Territories to Britain in 1898 was not necessarily because they feared the loss of opportunity to squeeze the weak:

> Tax farmers in the 包攬 business gained by and large at the expense of the government, not of the tax-payers who paid the tax farmers generally no more than what they had to pay under direct collection.[36]

Landownership

The county was a stronghold of lineage settlement, the best and largest areas of agricultural land being in the hands of a few major kinship groups. Krone states that:

> The villages in the plain of San-Keaou are almost exclusively inhabited by four clans — Man 文, Mak 麥, Tsang 曾, and Chang 陳. The villages inhabited by other clans are of no importance, and gradually either become absorbed in the more powerful clans, or are ruined by their hostility, and forced to remove to some other part of the country.[37]

San-Keaou 新橋 is in the north-west of Xin'an, but the same pattern was discernible throughout the county, and for the area of the present New Territories has been well documented.[38]

Corporate ownership of land was one of the foundations of lineage power and some lineages were heavily endowed with landholding trusts. Potter reports that 93 per cent of land belonging to one New Territories village in the 1960s was trust land, and Baker shows that in 1906, 52 per cent of the land of another lineage in the same area was owned corporately.[39] But it was a lineage's control over its individual members and trusts rather than the amount of land over which it had direct control which gave it its power. The one outstandingly wealthy trust in Baker's village owned some 52 acres in 1906, but the average size of trust holdings was only just over 3 acres.[40]

In Xin'an there was in fact very little concentration of landownership. Most of the farmers were small proprietors who worked with their own hands, aided by the rest of the family and seldom employing hired labourers. The average farm was probably not so large even as the 3-acre figure for trust holdings given above. Speaking of the New Territories, Hayes has said:

> Universal ownership was clearly shown by the land survey which followed the lease of 1898. This was carried out by surveyors and staff on loan from the Government of India, and was followed by a registration of titles which was enlivened by land courts which sat to determine possession in disputed cases.....
>
> At Shek Pik and Fan Pui in 1958 out of sixty-six families four owned between 3-4 acres, nine between 2-3 acres, nineteen between 1-2 acres, fourteen owned between a half to one acre, twelve owned between a quarter to a half, and eight between .10 to .25 acres. Except a few late arrivals, therefore, every family owned land of its own. The position was much the same as in 1898.[41]

The typical farm consisted of several scattered plots, not unlike the pre-enclosure farm in seventeenth-century England. It was undoubtedly uneconomical, a great amount of time and energy being spent in carrying implements, fertilizers and harvest between the farmer's home and the various plots. Land also was wasted in the boundaries and footpaths between different plots and in irrigation channels which sometimes had to go long distances, otherwise unnecessary, past neighbours' fields. The chief cause of the constant fragmentation of land was the traditional Chinese system of inheritance by which a father's holding was divided equally among his sons.

Fishing

Fishing was the principal occupation of the Tanka and the Hoklo, and probably stood second to agriculture in the county's economy. No statistics are available for the number of people engaged in the fishing industry in the period under consideration, and one of the edicts reproduced in the gazetteer speaks of 'incalculable numbers' of boat people.[42] Land-dwellers were also involved in fishing, either part-time as stake-net operators along the coastline or full-time as brackish or freshwater pond-fish farmers. There were 2,698 *mu* of fishponds registered in the county, many of them doubtless in the Deep Bay area of the New Territories where they are today.[43]

> The inhabitants along the coast support themselves principally by fishing. Hundreds of old men, women, and children, may be seen on the extensive flats left by the receding tide, collecting the small fishes, crabs, and other animals which have been stranded; with these they season their rice. The able-bodied men are with their boats at sea.[44]

The harvest to be won from the sea was a rich one, for the coastal waters teemed with many kinds of fish. Chapter Three gives thirty-five different varieties, some of which have several subtypes, and not all of which are edible. Eight kinds of shellfish are listed, amongst them the jellyfish as well as shrimps, crabs and oysters. Notes are made of the times of year when the fish are to be caught, the methods of catching them, and any special uses or way of preparation as food:

> The Yellow Croaker 黃花魚 ...is caught in deep water from the 9th to the 11th month. The fishermen listen for the noise of the shoals in the evening, then surround them with nets and so catch them....
>
> The Sea Catfish 鯐魚 can be as big as several tens of catties. They appear in the second month of spring and look like a black cloud. The fishermen surround the shoal which can be thousands of feet long. When one fish has been speared, another comes to drink its blood and can in turn be speared, and so they are caught in a continuous chain. Catching one means catching a myriad.

> The Flying Fish 飛魚 has a small body with long fins....at night it sees the fishermen's lights and comes flying on board. Very good when boiled.
>
> The Globefish 河豚....has poison in its saliva....and if not properly prepared can be fatal to man. In autumn it is at its best, a warming food and good for the stomach, but it is still highly dangerous and it is wise not to eat it at all.[45]

The life of the fishermen was hard and uncertain. The summer months with the ever-threatening typhoons were a major hazard, but equally dangerous were the men who chose to prey upon shipping. With no protection from a state which had little interest in what was beyond its coastline, the boat people were forced to look to their own resources. They formed themselves into fleets called *gupeng* 罟朋 and were probably as often predatory on their own kind as they were on the fish.[46]

Every such fleet had an 'administrative boat' 料船 following it in charge of storing and salting fish and preparing food for the fishermen of the entire group. But these fleets which originated partly perhaps in the desire for protection against pirates seem to have led to the further growth of piracy: a group of fishing boats could easily form the nucleus of a pirate syndicate should circumstances so permit or dictate:

> Guangdong has many brigands and its seas swarm with pirates, most of whom are Tanka. Their boats ply the waters at will in larger or smaller numbers .... Sometimes a few nets, and sometimes over ten nets form one fleet and these fleets have boats going out with them for the salting of fish. Whenever an opportunity presents itself they take to piracy and prey on merchant ships. When harvests are being reaped they rush into the fields and cut down the grain and farmers who wish to save their crops have to offer them money to go back to sea. That is how vicious they are.[47]

It was to try to control such piracy that at the end of the Ming dynasty *baojia* 保甲 registration was proposed for the boat people,[48] though it is unlikely that it was ever implemented.

The fish were brought ashore to be sold at coastal markets. The principal fishing centres seem to have been Xixiang 西鄉 , Fuyong 伏涌 (probably an error for 福永), Bitou 碧頭 and Gui'de 歸德 ,[49] but other coastal anchorages and markets abounded. Centred on the four places named above were to be found the *she* 社 which had formerly been under the Dongguan County fish-duty station but were transferred to Xin'an in 1573. These *she* were the divisions of the countryside for collection of fish-tax,[50] but the income from the tax was not high:

> Even in the fourteenth century the system was impractical. The fishermen, who moved about from place to place, found it easy to evade the duties, and the local authorities could do little about it. By the late sixteenth century the fish duty was collected in a great variety of ways. In Yung-chou prefecture, Hukwang, for instance, there were six counties and one subprefecture. By 1571 only three of the counties continued to collect the duty from fishermen while the other four made it up from the land taxes. In general it seems certain that more counties adopted the latter approach than the former.[51]

The tax quota was set in 1687 at 241.161 taels of silver with a surcharge of 28.650 taels, a total of 269.811 taels per annum to be included in the overall totals of the land-taxes.[52]

Salt

Salt-making was in theory a monopoly of the government. In practice the government supervised the work of production while the distribution of salt was in the hands of licensed firms which operated according to regulations imposed by the government.

According to the gazetteer's section on the salt administration,[53] in 1369 the Ming dynasty had set up two salt superintendencies in Guangdong Province. One was on Hainan Island.[54] The other consisted of twelve production centres 場, four of which were in the area which later came to be Xin'an County, and of these by 1542 mergers had left just two, Gui'de Centre in the western half and Dongguan Centre administered from Nantou. Between them these two are said to have covered 209,916 *mu* (some 35,000 acres), more than half as much land as was being taxed for agriculture in the county. The figure seems extremely high, especially as there were fewer than 3,000 salt-workers registered for tax, but it is likely that the workforce would actually be much larger than just those registered.

There were 16 salterns, called *she* 社, under Gui'de Centre and 7½ salterns, called *zha* 柵, under Dongguan Centre. All were sited along the coastlines, some on the mainland others on islands, notably on Lantau. The salt was extracted from seawater by natural evaporation. The salt-fields

> are raised flat areas, enclosed by embankments about one foot in height. The floors of these are made very hard and smooth, being covered with chunam, into which pebbles are stamped, so that the crystals of salt can be collected without loss and without injury to the fields. These fields measure from thirty to fifty yards square; they are intersected by canals into which the sea water is admitted at high tide. From these canals the water is allowed to flow into the salt-fields, and cover them to the depth of about six inches; the communication with the canal is then shut off, so as to prevent the reflux of the water.

> In dry weather crystals begin to be formed as early as the second day, and if no rain interfere with the process of crystallization, on the third or fourth day the water may be drawn off till it is only one inch in depth, and on the fifth day, fair weather continuing, the salt may be collected.[55]

A second method of collection was by 'leaching', the brine being sprinkled onto loose soil and allowed to concentrate, then leached out with more sea water which was collected and evaporated off. A better quality salt was obtained by this method.[56]

Like agricultural land, salt-producing land was divided into three categories for taxation purposes, superior, medium, and inferior, depending on the degree of suitability of the area for the industry. In addition to the tax on salt fields, there was a tax on each worker engaged in the industry. And finally, firms undertaking the sale and distribution of salt must hold licences issued by the government.

In Gui'de Centre the salt-field tax was originally set at 0.003425, 0.003082 and 0.0023975 taels per *mu* per annum. In Dongguan Centre the equivalent three grades were 0.001875, 0.001437 and 0.0005639 taels per *mu*. These figures were all raised across the board by 0.02 taels in 1682, and then in 1737 it was decided to remit two-fifths of the tax on Gui'de and three-fifths on Dongguan. The tax load seems to have been generally very light, but it was a high-risk occupation because of the uncertain weather graph, and the industry seems to have gone into decline. In 1756 both centres were closed down, and in 1789 there came a recommendation to convert the salt pans into agricultural land, but

> the salt-fields were almost all in sandy or rocky areas and had been inundated with sea water for so long that it was very difficult to make them sweet enough to do duty as paddy fields.[57]

When the two centres were closed the salt trade was placed entirely in the hands of licensed merchants 埠 . Originally there had been four of these merchant organizations at Baishi 白石 , Nantou, Xixiang and Guxu 固戍 , but by the early nineteenth century only one remained, the Pengchengbu 彭城埠 based just outside Nantou.[58] The selling price of their salt was fixed at 0.007 taels per catty, and the organization paid an annual tax of 2,263.491 taels for their right to trade.

By 1859 Krone could report that:

> At present, in consequence of the large quantity of cheap salt imported from Hongkong, much smuggling goes on, and the people have greatly relaxed in their diligence to produce the amount due to government.[59]

But illegal dealing in salt certainly predated the birth of Hong Kong and the gazetteer notes the provision of six patrol boats to counteract smuggling.[60]

Markets

The economy of the country was little oriented to the outside world. It appears to have been if anything deficient in grain and had to buy from elsewhere.[61] Some of its salt and fish were presumably exported, but the old lucrative trade in incense had long been dead by the time the gazetteer was produced. In general the county must have been self-sufficient, having neither local specialities to export, nor any great need of exotic goods.

The movement of goods round the countryside would doubtless have been hampered both by the hilly nature of the terrain and by the lack of planned roads. There were two post-roads stretching from the county town eastwards to Dapeng and northwards to Dongguan,[62] but they were maintained for administrative not economic reasons. Probably like other routes they were no more than narrow paths paved with granite slabs.[63]

The list of markets 墟市 given in Chapter Two of the gazetteer gives some idea of where the economic centres of the county lay, but no information is offered as to the schedules or relative importance of the markets. We know from the Hong Kong New Territories area that markets met on three days of every ten-day lunar week. Shenzhen 深圳 was an intermediate level market and met on a 2-5-8 schedule, that is it was held on the 2nd, 5th, 8th 12th, 15th, 18th, 22nd, 25th and 28th days of the lunar month. Shihuxu 石湖墟, Shatoujiao 沙頭角, Yuanlang 元朗 and Dabu 大埔 were all standard markets dependent on Shenzhen, the former two meeting on a 1-4-7 schedule and the latter on 3-6-9.[64] Clearly Shenzhen was of major importance to the south-eastern area of Xin'an, but we have no such data for the rest of the county. The Krone article of 1859 and the Volonteri map of 1866 are both of some help, but neither really has sufficient detail.

Water transport was important in a district bordered by sea, and the list of ferries given in Chapter Seven provides a pointer to some significant centres of trade. That more defunct than operating services are noted[65] combines with the known slump in the salt trade to indicate that the early years of the nineteenth century were probably far from affluent for the county.

4. GOVERNMENT

The gazetteer is concerned above all, of course, with the administration of Xin'an County. The founding of the county, the centres of government, the ceremonies which aimed to strengthen and give colour to the authority of the officials, the qualifications and achievements of those officials and of those natives of the county who entered officialdom, the problems of administration which exercised the magistrate and his staff peculiarly in this county — on all these the gazetteer is strong.

Yet at the same time it is in this very field of administration that the gazetteer is weak. The inadequacy of the maps has already been pointed out, and the careful listing of all existing villages by name is made useless by the failure to give their locations. The maps of the 1688 and 1819 administrative divisions (Maps 7 & 8) were arrived at only with the greatest difficulty, and must be considered to be no more than rough approximations. A magistrate informed of an insurrection at Tianxin Village 田心村 would have had no easy way of deciding to which one he should dispatch troops, since there are four of them listed in Chapter Two, three in the Guanfu District.

There is no guidance to be found on linguistic problems, major headaches for the officials posted in from other provinces. Nor is there any indication of the existence of tax-farming nor even the briefest clue as to methods of tax-collection. And, perhaps even more important, the strength of the domination of the countryside by powerful lineages is ignored. The description of the administrative system is by no means complete.

Civil administration

Before 1573, the region we are dealing with was part of Dongguan, and the history of its administration then has to be sought in the gazetteers of that county. Throughout the sixteenth century pirates were active along the coast of China, and the southern half of Dongguan was so far away from the county seat that 'the Japanese and Western barbarian pirates were constantly able to gather to wreak havoc'.[1] Some local inhabitants petitioned the government to turn southern Dongguan into a separate county so that it could be controlled and defended more easily. The request was granted, and in 1573 Xin'an County came into existence with its yamen at Nantou. The name Xin'an (New Peace) was given to it, no doubt, in anticipation of the state of affairs which its creation was to bring about. Between 1666 and 1669, for reasons of military strategy much of the region was evacuated and the county re-incorporated into Dongguan, but from 1669 until the founding of the Chinese Republic in the twentieth century Xin'an was again a full county under Guangzhou Prefecture. Then, as Bao'an County 寶安縣 it survived until 1979 when it was finally abolished.[2]

Probably an increase in population was another contributing cause of the original separation of Xin'an from Dongguan.[3] Some 34,000 people were reckoned to live in the county when it was set up, and this had risen to 34,500 by 1582.[4] A massive decrease was brought about by the coastal evacuation of 1662 to 1669 of course, and thereafter it is impossible to discover how realistic the population figures given in the gazetteer were. Before the 'never raise taxes' decree of 1713, under-registration of population must be assumed,[5] while after that date over-registration is a strong possibility as an increase could be taken as a sign of good government. By 1818 the population was stated to be 226,000 civilians plus 13,000 under military registration.[6] When in 1898 J.H.S. Lockhart made a fact-finding tour prior to the lease of the New Territories, he estimated the population of the extension area to be just over 100,000.[7] Since the leased territory comprised the less heavily settled three-fifths of Xin'an, a total population figure of over 200,000 for the early nineteenth century does not seem unlikely.

Despite the fluctuations in population size the official administrative establishment remained almost constant throughout the county's history. In 1573 the civil officials consisted of the County Magistrate 知縣, a Director of Studies 教諭, an Assistant Director of Studies 訓導, an Assistant Magistrate for Guanfu District 官富巡檢 (not actually appointed until 1574), an Assistant Magistrate for Fuyong District 福永巡檢, a Chief of Police 典史, Supervisors 大使 for the salt administration's Dongguan and Gui'de centres, and Supervisors and a Collecting Officer 攢典 for the Dapeng and Yongying 永盈 granaries. Sixteen clerks were assigned to these officials.[8]

The posts of the two Granary Supervisors and their Collecting Officer did not remain for long, and the two salt administration posts were abolished in 1789. The post of Director of Studies lapsed in 1664, presumably because of the reduction in size of the population caused by the evacuations, but it was re-established in 1678, nine years after the return. The major change was the setting up in 1723 of a Deputy Magistrate 縣丞 at Dapeng, formerly a garrison town 守禦所.

A complete list of magistrates serving in Xin'an County up to 1819 is included in Chapter Five of the gazetteer. Their places of birth, the dates on which they took office, and their academic qualifications are all set out, while the work of those who were considered to have rendered service to the county in a special way is described further in individual biographies in Chapter Fourteen.[9] The average tenure of office was two and a half years, some magistrates serving for less than a year and one man achieving an unprecedented twelve year term from 1730 to 1741, so that even in the next century 'the people were still praising him'.[10]

The magistrates did not all hold the same qualifications. Fourteen of the ninety-six holders of the office had passed the high level *jinshi* degree, and thirty-eight the mid-ranking *juren*. Of the rest twenty-one had passed the lowest level *gongsheng* examinations, twelve had purchased or been otherwise awarded degrees, and eleven apparently had no degree at all.

> To check officials from utilizing existing personal contacts in the districts allocated to them, imperial regimes established the principle of avoidance. Under the laws of avoidance, a magistrate was not allowed to serve in the province in which his native district was situated, nor to serve in a district within 165 (Western) miles of his native district. In his first district post he would ordinarily be unfamiliar with its local customs, dialect and subordinate office personnel.[11]

True to these principles not one of the Xin'an magistrates came from Guangdong Province. As an anti-corruption measure avoidance can have been only partially effective, for linguistic problems were an effective barrier to an official's understanding of any graft which might be being practised by his subordinates. The edict of 1728 urging reform of the speech of Fujian and Guangdong provinces identified the problems, but could hardly have contributed to their solution.[12]

The other officials were less well qualified than the County Magistrate. The mid-ranking *juren* degree was held by only eight of the Directors of Studies and by three Assistant Directors of Studies. None of the Deputy Magistrates had better than a *gongsheng* degree, and fewer than half of the Assistant Magistrates had even a purchased degree to their names. The avoidance principle was observed in appointing most of these lower officials, though one of the Fuyong Assistant Magistrates did come from Guanfu District, and quite a number of the education officials were from Guangdong Province — perhaps because it did not matter:

> The local educational officials held sinecures. The assistant district officials lacked authority. Their powers were extremely curtailed and their salaries and staff insignificant.[13]

An 1896 report on another part of Guangdong Province talks of a

> sub-district deputy magistrate armed with an amount of authority that barely enables him to call in question the theft of a matchbox.[14]

And Krone, who had little respect for the mid-nineteenth century mandarin, relates an anecdote which testifies to the impotence of the Fuyong Assistant Magistrate of that time:

> The mandarin .... had not, as far [as] I know, during a period of several years, more than one case brought before him for decision; in this instance he was both plaintiff and judge — the criminal being a youth who was caught stealing fruit in his garden. Anxious to give the people an impression of his severity, he had the prisoner scourged, and continued the punishment till he was obliged to desist for fear that the prisoner might die. This excessive severity was caused by his vexation at not being able to get a groan, or a cry, or a prayer for pardon, from the culprit, as a proof of his power. This solitary act of justice of the mandarin was much laughed at by the people.[15]

The Fuyong Assistant Magistrate, like his Guanfu colleague, could call on the assistance of a princely total of two archers when he needed to exert his authority.[16] But if the trappings of the minor officials were but lowly, the same was not true of the County Magistrate. His yamen was the most imposing building in the county:

> The yamen is in the centre of the city and faces south. Its heart is the main hall with below it a terrace surrounded by a balustrade. Below that again is the approach road with its arches inscribed with moral sayings. Flanking the road are the clerks' quarters, and at the head of it the ceremonial gate, outside which to the east lie the Earth God shrine, the Guest Welcoming hall, and the new granary, while to the west ....[17]

The description goes on to list granaries, leisure quarters, the gaol, a garden, the kitchen, and more. By contrast the Chief of Police had to be content with just the following:

> The Chief of Police's office is to the left of the main hall of the magistracy. It has a main hall, with a guest room on the left, a bedroom behind, and the clerk's room in front.[18]

The duties of the County Magistrate as head of the local hierarchy of officials were of a very wide range:

> An imperially sponsored source of the late eighteenth century listed his duties as

> 'superintending the government of a district, regulating its taxes and labor services, hearing and administering its legal suits, promoting education and culture, and controlling its customs.' It said that 'all help for the aged, sacrifice to spirits, provision for scholars, and regulation of study he is personally responsible for and diligently manages.'[19]

'Superintending the government' of the county meant that all matters civil and military came within the Magistrate's purview. His was the key role in bringing together the aspirations of government and people. To play that role successfully he had to be seen to work for the people under his rule while at the same time he must be conscious always that he was the representative of the State and bound to work for its good.

> The immense geographical expanse of the empire and its limited facilities for communication and transportation, coupled with the illiteracy and political indifference of the overwhelming majority of the inhabitants, rendered it exceedingly difficult even to make known the laws and decrees of the government, to say nothing of enforcing them or carrying them out. The district magistrate, who was supposed to administer directly to the people's needs, had under his jurisdiction an area often over a thousand square miles in extent. With a total of roughly 1,500 magistrates .... there was on the average one magistrate for 100,000 inhabitants (calculated on the basis of the 1749 official figures) or 250,000 (1819 official figures). The magistrate was so overburdened with a wide range of vaguely prescribed duties that he had little time or facilities to do any of them well, if indeed he had the intention or capacity to do so at all.[20]

To help him to preserve order the Magistrate had a force of yamen runners 衙役, who acted as policemen, messengers, gaolers and coroners as well as caretakers, musicians and general dogsbodies.[21] No details of the number of runners employed in the county are given in the Xin'an gazetteer, but the provincial gazetteer for 1822 says that Xin'an had a quota of eighty-three lictors and guards with a total annual salary bill of 498 taels,[22] which works out at six taels per man, the national norm.[23] It is clear from the comments of Krone and from the frequency of the bandit attacks mentioned in Chapter Thirteen that this band of runners was inadequate to maintain the peace, and a succession of Magistrates was forced to call on help from the military and from higher authorities.[24]

In seeking that help the County Magistrate relied on the official postal system, set up and maintained empire-wide for the transmission of state documents. A series of trunk roads emanated from the capital at Beijing, and local systems were keyed into these.[25] There were two separate routes from Xin'an City.[26]

The more important one went northwards to Dongguan and from there appears to have proceeded via Zengcheng 增城 to link up with the prefectural and provincial capital of Guangzhou.[27] The other route went eastwards to Dapeng, and provided the necessary land link with the second most important military and civilian administrative centre of the county. Within the county boundaries both these routes were under the control of the Xin'an Magistrate, and a series of stations or staging posts was built along them at regular intervals. It would have taken about a day for messengers on foot to travel the 120 *li* to Dapeng, and to reach Beijing would have taken approximately sixty days on foot or about thirty-five days on horseback if there were urgency.[28]

For the people of a county the appointment of a new magistrate could mean peace and prosperity or harrassment and exploitation depending on the man chosen. Too often it probably meant neither, for the administrative load was too great for the appointee to carry effectively. In any case the county magistrate was the one man the people could have hopes of benevolent help from, and he was called by names which expressed that hope; names such as *difang guan* 地方官 'the local official', *qinmin zhi guan* 親民之官 'the official close to the people' and *fumu guan* 父母官 'the father and mother official'. Xin'an's situation was typical not only in terms of size of population at 1819, but probably also in the fewness of the really able men who had ever been set in charge of it.

Taxation

An important function of the local administration was the collecting of taxes for the state. Failure to achieve a high success rate in the collection could seriously affect the magistrate's career:

> A magistrate who failed to collect the proper quota of land-and-labor-service tax within a given time was subject to punishment, which was determined by the percentage of tax uncollected. If the uncollected portion was less than ten per cent, he was not entitled to promotion and was subject to forfeiture of one year's nominal salary. The punishment was demotion of one to four grades if the portion uncollected was ten, twenty, thirty, or forty per cent respectively. If he failed to collect more than fifty per cent, he was subject to dismissal.[29]

To ensure collection in Xin'an the magistrates resorted to tax-farming, as we have seen, though we have as yet no precise knowledge of the way in which the taxes were assembled and transported. Krone's article furnishes some evidence:

> When the Mandarins intend to levy the taxes, they announce their intention to the gentry of the villages, one or two weeks, or sometimes a month, before their arrival. They then make a progress through the district, accompanied by a suffi-

> cient force to protect themselves against large bands of robbers, which sometimes have the audacity to attack the tax-collectors if the escort be not strong.[30]

It seems likely that the officials of the four districts of the county were 'the Mandarins' referred to above, and that their personal overseeing of the tax collection through forays into the countryside was designed to increase the success rate and so make secure their own positions. The method became very common practice towards the end of the Qing dynasty.[31] Krone believed that it worked well:

> The amount of taxes and other duties I have not been able to ascertain. They are, however, with few exceptions, regularly paid.[32]

The total tax for which the county was assessed was 13,329.358 taels in a normal year, plus an additional 293.72 taels in a year with an intercalary month. Of this sum 597.847 taels (plus 41.793 taels in thirteen-month years) was kept back by the Magistrate as a handling charge; 1,371.96 taels (plus 70.028 in long years) was spent by him on official ceremonies of worship and on the regular salaries of the county officials and runners; and 1,060 taels he spent on supplementary salaries for the officials.[33] The rest was delivered immediately after collection to the provincial treasury.[34]

Law and order

The gazetteer has little to say on the subject of the law or of court cases decided in Xin'an, though the County Magistrate was responsible for investigating crime, and for hearing and judging criminal cases.[35] Some of the biographies of distinguished officials given in Chapter Fourteen indicate by whom justice was thought to have been fairly administered, but virtually no details are given.[36]

Education

Much more emphasis is placed on the exhortative, prophylactic role of the officials. Chapter Ten lays down the procedure for the *xiangyue* ceremony 鄉約 held twice a month, when the Sacred Edict 聖諭 of the Kangxi emperor was to be expounded to the populace.[37] Such clauses as 'Put an end to false accusations so as to make safe the innocent' and 'Do not conceal fugitives lest you become an accessory to crime' must have been popular texts with those charged with administering the law.[38]

The lecture ceremonies began with ritual kneelings and kotows (marks of respect for the throne rather than worship). The gazetteer does not indicate whether the lectures were actually given or not, but other sources suggest that in counties throughout China the observance was at best sporadic and in some places non-existent. The Abbé Huc travelled extensively in the early 1850s and reported:

> Now things are managed in a very different manner: there are indeed in all the localities places appointed where the Mandarins ought to instruct the people; they are called .... 'Hall of Holy Instructions'; but on the appointed day the Mandarin does but just walk in, smoke a pipe, drink a cup of tea, and walk out again. Nobody is there to listen to him, and if there were he would not trouble himself to say a word.[39]

Krone misunderstands the reason for the *xiangyue*, but says of Xin'an:

> A small public Library exists at the residence of the district mandarin; the books it contains have been presented to the province by different emperors, and consist chiefly of *Commentaries on the Classics*, or *Treatises on Ethics*. They are intended for the instruction of the people; but as it would be inconvenient to allow the people in general free access to them, it is ordered that the mandarin should assemble the people on certain days, and read and explain the contents of these books to them. For the last twenty years, at any rate, no mandarin has, to my knowledge, attempted the performance of these duties; and as the collection is but poorly cared for, the worms alone derive any advantage from it.[40]

Chapter Nine describes the twice-yearly banquet 鄉飲酒 held by the Magistrate to honour the aged and the worthy of the county and so to encourage the people to follow suit.[41] And Chapters Nineteen and Twenty note official recognition of people with virtues much esteemed by Confucian orthodoxy.[42]

The role of political propagandist merged with that of the educator, and the County Magistrate and the gazetteer were both much concerned with education. The whole of Chapters Nine, Fifteen, Sixteen and Seventeen are devoted to matters of education in the county, and the subject receives frequent treatment in the writings and biographies of the magistrates as well as in the sections on edicts, on public buildings and elsewhere.

In Chapter Five are listed the names of fifty-seven Directors of Studies for the county, though there is a gap of thirty-odd years in the Qianlong period when 'owing to mildew damage the records are unreadable'.[43] Fifty-three Assistant Directors of Studies are listed, again with a gap in the Qianlong records caused by mildew. Both the Director of Studies and the Assistant Director of Studies were technically responsible to the Provincial Director of Studies, and the provision of all educational facilities was supposed to be in the care of these men, but in practice the County Magistrate was frequently left with the task, as the biographical section of the gazetteer testifies.[44]

Chapter Nine lists the books received from the state by the local education officials for the library from 1723 onwards. They include multiple copies of various imperial edicts, of regulations governing education and of standard classical works such as the Four Books (the *Analects of Confucius*, the *Great Learning*, the *Doctrine of the Mean*, and the *Mencius*):

> The government allowed the schools almost no liberty in formulating their programs of instruction. Practically everything was regulated so that the instruction given would be subservient to the interest of the dynasty. Curricula were determined largely by the subject matter covered by the state examinations. Official textbooks were selected, compiled, and distributed by the government, which virtually fixed the circumference as well as the center of literary instruction.[45]

Also in Chapter Nine are given the student quotas for the county. Eight students were to be allowed to pass the *shengyuan* 生員 'licentiate' degree at each of the examinations which were held by the Provincial Director of Education. There were two such examinations in every three years, one held after the *sui* 歲 examinations and one after the *ke* 科 examinations.[46] A quota of twenty *linsheng* 廩生 'salaried licentiates' were to receive the government stipend. The gazetteer does not say what that stipend was, but the provincial gazetteer for 1822 states that it was standard for all parts of the province at 2.4 taels per man per annum.[47] Another twenty licentiates were to be in the *zengsheng* 增生 'additional licentiate' quota; though they did not receive a stipend they did benefit from some preferential treatment. The remainder of those who had passed the *shengyuan* degree were known as *fusheng* 附生 'supplementary licentiates' and were not limited as to number.[48] The quota for 'military licentiates' 武生員 was also eight per examination, but only one examination was held every three years; that is, there was no military examination after the *ke* examinations. Additional quotas for Hakka students were laid down in 1716 and revised in 1735 and 1802.[49]

The purpose of the *sui* and *ke* examinations was to select from the licentiates those who were fit to take part in the provincial examinations for the *juren* degree, but the candidates could suffer demotion or even dismissal on the strength of their performance.[50] Chapter Fifteen lists all the successful civil examinees from the county at the different levels higher than licentiate. Village of origin and the year when successful are given for most entries. Chapter Sixteen lists similarly those from the county who passed military examinations, and Chapter Seventeen gives rather less full information on men who had obtained academic degrees by purchase rather than by examination.

We cannot tell from the gazetteer how stiff the competition for these quota places was, nor how many attended schools or achieved any degree of literacy.

Some areas of China were traditionally famous for their production of scholars, but Xin'an was not one of them. Its examination pass quota was very nearly the lowest of any county of Guangzhou Prefecture and considerably lower than that of the most advantaged counties. Only Hua Xian 花縣 with a quota of seven passes was lower than Xin'an. Three other counties were at the same level, one county had fourteen, two had fifteen, one had eighteen and five counties had quotas of twenty passes each.[51] There is evidence that the fixed quotas were in some measure at least a reflection of the intellectual assertiveness of county populations,[52] and Xin'an's low quota may therefore be taken as an indication of a weak cultural life.

Xu Sun, who had served as County Magistrate, wrote that Xin'an's inhabitants 'are farmers and fishermen, but they are not unmindful of study'.[53] None the less it was from him and other outsiders that the impetus for resuscitating the long-dead academy had to come; and according to the 1822 provincial gazetteer Xin'an was among the least well provided with academies in Guangdong, some counties supporting a large number of institutions — Xiangshan 香山, for example, had ten.[54] The list of seven charity schools 義學 in Chapter Nine also makes depressing reading where five are marked 'now defunct' 今廢, one built in 1694 had long been derelict before being converted as a temple in 1805, and only one appears to have been functioning.

The disruptive effects of the seventeenth century coastal evacuations may partly explain this poor academic provision, but there is another factor which should be taken into account. The Xin'an countryside was dominated by large lineages which were by local standards wealthy and powerful. Many, if not all, of these lineages maintained schools for the education and advancement of their own members,[55] but such schools did not figure in the gazetteer records, presumably because they were not open to all comers. In fact, then, wealthier inhabitants of the county were receiving an education in these schools and since they were the people who would otherwise have sought education elsewhere there was perhaps less need for county-run institutions. One private school which does receive mention is the Liying school 力瀛書齋 set up by Deng Fuxie at Jintian.[56] And County Magistrate Xu Sun (with more hope than accuracy) maintains that:

> despite being in a remote corner of the land there is not a family or community without its school, and it is by this means that culture and education have become so widespread.[57]

It is doubtful whether the village schools gave a very high standard of education even at their best.

Chapter Seven under the subheading 'School' 學校 talks of the 'school-temple' 學宮 , but there is no mention of students or teachers:

> Originally a school as well as a ritual and administrative center, the school-temple eventually lost its teaching function altogether. Even as the system of government schools was being fleshed out during the Sung period, the shift in function was under way. By late Ming, school-temples were primarily concerned with the annual official Confucian rites and with administrative tasks related to the examination system. As the government schools were articulated to form a system of loci for Confucian activities through which central control could be exercised the need developed for places of genuine teaching and study. In broad perspective, it was the academies that came to fill this need.[58]

The school-temple in Xin'an had clearly become precisely the above kind of ritual venue,[59] and the gazetteer elsewhere commonly refers to it as the *Wen Miao* 文廟 'Temple for Civil Rites'.

In 1694 County Magistrate Ding Tangfa had built the Bao'an Academy,[60] but by 1819 both that and the later Wengang Academy founded by County Magistrate Duan Xiansheng in 1724 had long been defunct. (The site of the latter in Wutong Street in the west part of the city was still there.)[61] Work on the Fenggang Academy 鳳岡書院 began in 1803 at the place where the old salt administration office had stood, and it was completed in 1806.[62] The endowments of land given by Liu Zhuanghua and by Liao Jiuwo[63] to the Wengang Academy were transferred to the new institution and with other endowments they amounted to a total income of 799.545 taels of silver. After payment of essential charges there remained 348.214 taels which could be spent on the salary of the resident teacher, on monthly provisions for students, on congratulatory banquets and so on.[64]

> The growth of *shu-yüan* [academies] in late imperial times also reflected the steadily increasing prominence of the examination system. With the government's growing reliance on examinations as the chief means of recruiting bureaucrats, and with the construction of examination sheds in virtually every capital throughout the empire, higher education inevitably focused more sharply on preparation for the imperial examinations. *Shu-yüan*, originally places of free discussion among literati and local officials, and in some respects centers of learning for learning's sake despite their de facto role in training schoolteachers, began to place increasing emphasis on training students to pass the examinations. Classical education, formerly an end in itself in terms of social standing, now became a means toward the ultimate status symbols — the graduate degrees of *chü-jen* [*juren*] and *chin-shih* [jinshi], attainable only through the imperial examinations.[65]

Chapter Fifteen shows the results of Xin'an's educational effort in terms of these 'ultimate status symbols'. Between 1573 and 1819 sixty-two men became *juren* and ten of those went on to pass the *jinshi* degree. Humble Hua Xian in the same period produced just four *jinshi*,[66] but Xiangshan achieved fourteen, neighbouring Dongguan seventy and Shunde well over a hundred.[67]

Relief

The already privileged literati were not the only recipients of government funding. The county also had the means of caring for the disadvantaged. Chapter Eleven contains a section on relief[68] and shows that a home for the blind and an asylum for the insane were maintained (though since both had been built in 1573 and no mention is made of restoration they must have been in a very dilapidated state). There were earmarked funds for the relief of those in special need, two burial grounds for disposing of unclaimed corpses, and granaries kept against harvest failure. Krone, noting that the gazetteer entries on relief are 'minutely detailed', remarks

> But it is well known that the poor and destitute derive little or no benefit from these sources, except the shelter against the wind and rain afforded them by the dilapidated tenements which are provided for them, and in which they may, without annoyance or maltreatment, consume the food which they have been able to procure by begging throughout the day.[69]

No details of the administration of the relief measures are given in the gazetteer, though it is likely that local gentry were expected both to contribute to and to supervise the work.[70] This probably applied as much in normal times as in emergencies such as droughts, typhoons and bandit attacks. An example of extraordinary relief measures during a pirate invasion in 1630 is given in Chapter Thirteen.[71]

Official religious practices

Less mundane was the duty of the local officials to intercede with the supernatural on behalf of the county's population. The County Magistrate had a formal relationship with the City God 城隍 which was as important to the county as was at state level the relationship of the Emperor with Heaven:

> Just as the magistrate protects the city from visible dangers, the god guards it from spiritual enemies and influences. His duties are multifarious; he acts as governor, judge, magistrate, tax-collector and coroner, and has a retinue of secretaries and attendants. He controls the demons of his district, and can compel them to release his territory from drought and plagues. The magistrate is the *yang* 陽 official, the

> Ch'eng Huang 城隍 is the *yin* 陰 official. They are of equal rank. The magistrate offers incense as a matter of courtesy. They are jointly responsible for the welfare of the city. In case the magistrate has a case he cannot manage, he goes to the Ch'eng Huang, who is able to see what he cannot, for help and council. In case the city needs rain the Ch'eng Huang's image is carried out, that he may see the need and help.[72]

The first duty of a newly appointed Xin'an County Magistrate, even before going to his yamen, was to visit the City God and make sacrifice to him, and thereafter he repeated the visit twice a month.[73] Regular twice-monthly visits of worship were made also to the Temple of the Empress of Heaven 天后 , a goddess of great importance to the boat people and coastal population of the county;[74] to the Shrine of the Earth God 土地祠 ;[75] and, most elaborate of all in ceremonial worship, to the Temple for Civil Rites 文廟 . Chapter Ten devotes much space to a description of the official rites, the days on which each ceremony was to be held, the prayers to be recited, the music to be played, the offerings to be made, the dances to be performed, if any, and the order of procedure. Even the exact measurements and colour of the spirit-tablet of Confucius (the chief recipient of the worship) are laid down.[76] Less frequent was the religious ceremony performed by the officials at the time of solar eclipses;[77] and sometimes special ceremonies were necessary, such as praying for rain, or holding memorial services for the dead, or praying for relief from typhoons and other visitations.[78]

Military system

> A magistrate, although a civil official, also had to defend the city in an uprising or a foreign invasion. Failure to do so would incur dismissal and physical punishment.[79]

There are many examples in the gazetteer of County Magistrates' concern with and even participation in military affairs. Strictly speaking the army units stationed in the county were responsible to a military hierarchy under the Provincial Commander-in-Chief in Guangzhou,[80] but it appears that in practice they worked in co-operation with, if not actually under the command of, the County Magistrate.

Chapter Five gives details of the military establishment of the county, and the same information is duplicated in Chapter Eleven which is largely devoted to military matters.[81] Chapter Six lists the names of the officers who served in the county, many of whom came from Guangdong Province, and not a few even from Xin'an itself. Clearly the avoidance rule which applied to civil officials was not enforced in the military sphere. As in some other parts of the gazetteer there are several references to mildew damage as the reason for incomplete listings. An unusual section at the end of the chapter gives the names of the two patrol lieutenants and four patrol sergeants in post at Dapeng at the time of going to press, but does not name other incumbent officers.[82]

The disposition of the forces operating in the county was almost entirely coast-oriented, history having taught that the greatest security menace came from the sea, whether in the form of Japanese and Chinese pirates or Western traders and adventurers.[83] Indeed, as we have seen, it was this sea-borne danger that was given as the reason for the establishing of Xin'an County as an administrative unit in 1573, and it was the same problem which led to the evacuations of the coastal area in 1662 and 1664. The coastal defence map (Map 6) given in the gazetteer shows clearly, for all its inaccuracy, how the coast was lined with signal stations, forts and guard-posts.

From Chapter Eleven it can be seen that major fortifications existed near Nantou, on Lantau Island, at Kowloon, Tuoneng and at two sites near Chiwan, while the administrative cities of Nantou and Dapeng were also fortified. These posts were manned by twenty or thirty men each, and between them mounted 287 cannon, some of cast iron and some of wrought iron. Of the eight signal stations 墩台 listed, one had been abandoned and four are marked 'become a guard-post'. Two sergeants and two corporals were distributed among the stations, but there is no indication of how many other troops were deployed. One of the seven dyke watch-posts 塘房 had been converted to a guard-post, the remaining six having a complement of four soldiers each. Six camps 營盤 are listed, one abandoned, three converted to guard-posts, and the remaining two still operating, with one of them under the command of a lieutenant. Most numerous of all were the guard-posts 汎房 of which there were fifteen in addition to those converted from other functions. Six of them had a total complement of twenty-five locally recruited men, a corporal and a sergeant, but there are no figures for the rest.[84] Additional to these military posts were the various postal stations strung along the two routes to Dapeng and to the border with Dongguan County. They were manned by a total of twenty-seven courier soldiers.[85]

Nantou and Dapeng were the headquarters of the two battalions 營 into which the forces were divided.[86] The Xin'an Battalion comprised one thousand men under the command of a major 遊擊 , and the Dapeng Battalion had a strength of eight hundred men commanded by a lieutenant-colonel 參將 . The annual cost of maintaining the forces amounted to 25,386 taels plus 6,739 *dan* of rice and 23,822 bundles of hay.[87] The scales of pay are not given, but the 1822 edition of the provincial gazetteer shows that a lieutenant-colonel drew some 743 taels a year (including allowances for administrative expenses, the promotion of incorruptibility, etc.), a major received 631 taels, a cavalryman 24 taels plus 3.6 *dan* of rice, an infantryman 18 taels plus 3.6 *dan*, and the humble patrol guard 守兵 12 taels plus 3.6 *dan*.[88] The figures do not quite gell with the declared establishment and pay totals, and seem to indicate either that the forces were understrength or perhaps that some of the officers at least were drawing less than their allotted salary because of having only acting posts.[89] In any case it is quite possible that the established strength was not reflected in the true number of men under arms. Krone records that:

> The three forts above mentioned are ordered to have a garrison of twenty men, and to mount six guns each. I have visited these three places, but found neither guns nor soldiers, and the places themselves showed no signs of fortification, save a dilapidated wall.
>
> The guard stations should be furnished with from two to six soldiers each; they are scattered over the whole western part of the country, and are intended to serve as a check against the frequent highway robberies. I never found one of these stations occupied by soldiers.[90]

It should be remembered that Krone was writing forty years after the publication of the gazetteer and that these had been hard and debilitating years for China, so that the situation might indeed have deteriorated markedly from that described in 1819. Yet Davis, another writer who knew the south coast of China at first hand, wrote as early as 1836:

> The abuses and malversation on the part of the military officers intrusted with funds for the provision of soldiers, appear to be frequent; and there is reason to suppose that some of the assumed militia of China are little better than men of straw, whose alloted funds are misapplied, if not after the example, yet in the manner of that eminent commander Sir John Falstaff. It must have been to some such system that our embassy in 1816 was indebted for the ludicrous scenes exhibited in its progress. The Emperor's edicts ordained that the troops should wear 'an imposing aspect'; but, on approaching a town or station, numbers of fellows might be seen scouring along the banks of the river, laden with jackets and accoutrements, which were clapped on the backs of those who had been pressed for the occasion, and who betrayed, from under their assumed habiliments, the primitive dirt and rags of their condition.[91]

If the land forces were less than impressive it appears that the navy was even worse. Chapter Twelve begins with the axiom that coastal defence is the most important aspect of military administration,[92] but proceeds to chronicle the degeneration of the naval forces in the county. In the mid-Ming dynasty there were more than fifty ships in the fleet. These were the heady days when Wang Hong was able to engage and defeat a Portuguese expedition.[93] By 1961 there were 112 ships, but thereafter numbers fell rapidly and in 1819 there were seven ships under Xin'an Battalion and seven under Dapeng, a total of only fourteen.[94] Yet it is clear that the need for vigorous maritime defence was as urgent as ever: Chapter Thirteen mentions serious pirate troubles less than a decade before the gazetteer was published,[95] and the potentially hostile ships of Britain, France, Portugal and other nations were more and more frequently sailing up the Pearl River to Guangzhou. Krone, typically, has a disparaging anecdote to relate in order to show the Xin'an administration in a poor light:

> I have not been able to ascertain how many war-junks the Hip-toi has under his command at the various stations of the district....[The gazetteer] only says they are of the utmost importance to guard against the French and other barbarians. Several of the war-junks usually anchor at Namtow [Nantou], others a little to the N.W. of Ku-shu [Guxu]. The Mandarin at Fuk-wing [Fuyong] has one war-junk at his disposal, but his revenue not being enough to support the expense, he was in the habit of letting out the vessel for hire for mercantile purposes. The hirers however converted it into a pirate boat, and it was seized by the Chi-yuen [County Magistrate], and the Fuk-wing mandarin had to bribe his superior officer to avoid further punishment and degradation.[96]

The Assistant Magistrate's implication in piracy does not appear to have been particularly unusual. An edict reproduced in the gazetteer rails against the involvement of the coastal guards in illegal and anti-social activities.[97] On the one hand there were fishermen who, given the opportunity, would become pirates,[98] and on the other there were officials and soldiers who would turn to illicit gain. Government in Xin'an was not easy.

Local government

In practice the county administration had little to do with the everyday life of the population: there were so few officials and so little provision for carrying their authority to the mass of the people. How, for example, could the Guanfu Assistant Magistrate control 495 villages with his two archers? The only official answer was the *baojia* 保甲 system in which groups of households were registered as mutual responsibility units. Ten households were known as a *pai* 牌, ten *pai* made a *jia* 甲 and ten *jia* a *bao* 保. Each group appointed a headman. Ostensibly it was a means of population registration and crime control which was to be organized by the people themselves, and which was to feed into the government system at the level of the *bao* headman; but seen from the viewpoint of the ordinary man it was an attempt to control the population through mutual suspicion and fear. Headmen tended to be either grossly incompetent or heavily corrupt, and the system was extremely difficult to work with any degree of efficiency despite repeated official attempts to put it on a proper footing.[99] In Xin'an successive magistrates bent their minds to the problems of implementing the *baojia*,[100] but there is no reason to suppose that it was any more or less effective here than elsewhere.

Local government, in fact, was very much left in the hands of the people themselves, villages and lineages organizing their own educational facilities, their own relief measures, their own defences against bandits and hostile neighbours, and their own religious activity.[101] Economic, political, social and religious life was carried on for the most part without reference to the central government system, and hence receives little mention in the gazetteer.

Part Two
Translated Passages

TRANSLATED PASSAGES

The following fifty passages of translation from the 1819 gazetteer. vary in length: some are complete sections from the original, but many are excerpts only. Where brackets are used it indicates that the original text is in a smaller typeface. Page number references are to the 1974 Taiwan reprint edition.

CONTENTS

Chapter Five:

T.17 Civil establishment.

Chapter Seven:

T.18 Walled and moated cities.
T.19 Military offices.
T.20 The school.
T.21 Temples.

Chapter Eight:

T.22 Population.
T.23 Land-tax.

Chapter Nine:

T.24 The Xiangyin banquet.
T.25 Hakka examination quota.
T.26 The Fenggang Academy.

Chapter Ten:

T.27 Public lectures.
T.28 Saving the sun.
T.29 Taking up office.

Chapter Eleven:

T.30 Military establishment.
T.31 Charities administration.
T.32 Relief granaries.
T.33 Postal stations.

Chapter Twelve:

T.34 Coastal defences.
T.35 The fleet.

Chapter Thirteen:

T.36 Natural disasters.
T.37 Bandits.
T.38 The evacuation.

Chapter Fourteen:

T.39 Officials and their good works.

T.1

Notes on the revision of the gazetteer
重修新安縣志凡例

p.11

Our Emperors have repeatedly issued edicts severely warning us to take to heart the meaning and intentions of the law. The old gazetteer has not been brought up to date since 1688, but now we have respectfully and carefully edited it, adding and correcting so as to make clear the law.

The history of development of the county provides the framework of the book, but in the old gazetteer it was included in the geographical section where it was in parts clear and in parts confused. Here we have carefully revised it and placed it in a section of its own.

While geographical position is found by consulting the heavens, the actual county area is terrestrial, so the 'Heavens' chapter of the old gazetteer has now been incorporated in the 'Topography' section.

A gazetteer should be firmly based on maps. Xin'an has sea on three sides and coastal defence is particularly important. Therefore to the maps given in the old gazetteer we have added a coastal defence map so that it may be seen where lie the strategic points to be guarded.

The 'Official Buildings' chapter of the old gazetteer has been renamed 'Buildings'.

The chapters of the old gazetteer called 'Taxation', 'Ceremonial', and 'Military and Punitive' have all been included in the 'Administration' section.

Xin'an is a coastal county. While all is happily now peaceful, yet we should not forget past events and we must take care to strengthen our defences and be prepared against disaster. To this end we have specially created a 'Coastal Defences' chapter.

In the old gazetteer 'Famous Officials' were entered in the 'People' chapter. Now there is a separate 'Officials and their Good Works' chapter.

There are thirteen sections 門 [1] in addition to the Premier Chapter. To the Premier Chapter of collected edicts we would not presume to add a preface, but each of the other thirteen has been provided with a short introduction explaining the reasons for its inclusion.

The old gazetteer was very muddled, contained a vast number of errors and omissions, and was generally imperfectly organized. In this edition we have looked carefully at and re-edited the arrangement of sections, and we have added as much new material as we thought desirable.

It is well over a hundred years since the old gazetteer was revised in 1688, and there is a multitude of matters which ought to be included in this edition. In completing it in just three months we are painfully aware that some omissions are inevitable.

T.2

Opening up waste-land (AD 1723)
諭開墾

p.23

From the commencement of Our reign We have busied Ourselves night and day with whatever would advance the livelihood of Our people, and nowhere more assiduously than in planning and estimating. We are concerned that with the state having been at peace for many years, the population has increased and the produce of the land is only barely sufficient to support it. When there is a shortfall in the harvest the people have difficulty in finding anything to eat. In future as the population increases daily what will they live off? Only by opening up waste-land will the people be helped. But hitherto there have been abuses in the procedure. Officials at county, prefectural, provincial and viceregal levels have all demanded squeeze and unofficial extra fees, so that the cost of opening waste-land has been even greater than that of buying ready-cultivated land, and the people fear to come forward to take it up. It is shameful to leave fertile land uncultivated. From now on wherever there is waste-land let the people measure it off, open it up and report their claims themselves. The local officials must not demand bribes of them nor may yamen staff put difficulties in their way. In accordance with the tax regulations on new land, irrigated fields shall become liable to tax after six years and non-irrigated after ten years. Let prefectural and county officials who succeed in persuading the populace to open up sizeable areas of waste-land be recommended for advancement and so too governors, viceroys and senior officials whose leadership results in the opening of large areas. This is to ensure that no space will be wasted and that there will be enough land for the people. So may Our desire to give the people prosperity and abundance be satisfied.

T.3

The people of Fujian and Guangdong should pay more attention to agriculture (AD 1727)
諭閩廣百姓各務本業

p.30

There have been frequent complaints from viceroys and governors that Fujian and Guangdong provinces produce so little rice that they do not have enough to feed their own populations. Viceroy Gao Qizhou and Governor Yang Wenqian have sent in memorials pointing out that even in a year of good harvest there is barely sufficient in Guangdong for six months' consumption. We feel that there are bound to be some years of poor harvest when not enough rice is produced for local needs, but it is unreasonable for this situation to exist every year, even when the harvest has been good. It was unclear whether the fault lies in insufficient development of the available land, or in idleness and failure to put the necessary labour into farming, or in profiteers who scheme to sell the rice at inflated prices to foreigners. Yesterday we met and gave instructions on this to the chief ministers, and now the governor of Guangxi, Han Liangfu, has submitted a memorial stating that despite Guangdong's great size and ample population it still looks to Guangxi for its rice; that the Guangdong people seek money and profit, and plant much of their land with such things as longan, sugar-cane, tobacco and indigo with the result that they have wealth but no rice; and that Guangxi is a sparsely populated infertile province which cannot spare its produce for export to its neighbours. This memorial is in accord with the edicts We have issued in the past, and the reason for the shortage of food in Fujian and Guangdong is now clear. Let the viceroys and governors of these two provinces do all in their power to make the people realize that food is the most vital thing for them, and that they should concentrate on this basic necessity by devoting their energies to their fields. They must not neglect agriculture for the sake of making profit. The greatest merit lies in ignoring trivial pursuits and sticking to the hard life of the farmer. As for things like plantations and orchards, they should only be worked when there is surplus land and labour. How can it be right to look for short-term profit at the expense of neglecting the vital source of life? In case of emergency there is nothing to fall back on and aid has to be sought from the next province; and if the next province also happens to have a poor harvest, what then? The viceroys and governors in question must strive to understand and to give instructions to the people so that they may be fully alert to the dangers and work to overcome them. Then land will not be wasted and there will be no shortage of rice.

T.4

Standardize the speech of Fujian and Guangdong (AD 1728)
諭閩廣正鄉音

p.31

When officials go to their posts their speech must be such that everyone can understand them, otherwise they will be unable to fathom the mind of the populace or understand local affairs well enough to administer without making mistakes .... Of all the officials of every grade who come for audience it is only those from Fujian and Guangdong who when they speak have accents so strong that We cannot understand them. But if they are unable to make themselves understood to their superiors when they have been raised to the status of officials and been to the Board of Civil Appointment to rehearse the correct way of presenting a memorial, how will they ever make the common people understand them distinctly when they take office in another province and have to promulgate edicts and make judgements in court? When officials and subjects cannot understand each other the yamen clerks have to interpret, and then abuse is heaped upon abuse and many delays in doing business occur. The inability of the natives of these two provinces to communicate verbally with others does not only mean that those of them posted to serve in other provinces cannot be in sympathy with the people they govern, it means also that as a native populace they cannot understand the officials posted to govern them. When both high and low cannot communicate great inconvenience results. Language is a habit instilled from early childhood and cannot be changed all at once, but if the people are taught at a reasonable pace they will gradually come to be able to communicate. We order the viceroy and governors of Fujian and Guangdong to instruct the magistrates and education officials in all the prefectures and counties under their command to make it their business to teach the people to speak in a comprehensible manner and not in their accustomed local dialect. In that way We may clearly understand them when they deliver memorials at Our audiences, and when they go elsewhere to serve as officials they will be able to be in tune with the people they govern.

T.5

Imperial relief for the Tanka of Guangdong (AD 1729)

恩恤廣東蛋户

p.35

It is known that in Guangdong there are, as well as the people of the four classes,[2] a tribe of Yao barbarians called the Tanka, who have boats for homes and live by fishing. The waterways throughout the province are crammed with their craft and their population has risen to incalculable numbers. The Cantonese look down upon them as an inferior breed and do not allow them to live ashore.[3] The Tanka themselves do not dare enter into conflict with the land people. In fear they shelter away cramped up in their boats, never knowing the joy of a settled life: a most pitiful plight. The Tanka are a worthy people and should not be despised or outcast. They pay their taxes as fishermen and are no different from the rest of the population. Why just because of ancient local custom should they be discriminated against and made to keep on the move with no peace? The viceroy and governor shall communicate this edict to all officials so that they may carry out its instructions: any Tanka who are not physically strong may if they wish remain on their boats, but the able-bodied who can build houses or matsheds shall be permitted to reside in villages near the water and shall be entered on the *baojia* registers like the rest of the people so that they may be easily checked. Powerful families and local bullies must not seek ways to mistreat them or drive them away, and the officials should encourage the Tanka to open up waste-land and take up farming as good solid citizens, so justifying Our impartial regard for them.

T.6

Put an end to gambling (AD 1729)
詔禁賭博

p.36

From earliest days loafers and idlers have been anathema to those who rule. But gamblers are worse than mere idlers. They neglect their proper occupations and waste away their family fortunes, day by day their natures become more corrupt and their schemes more crooked. When fathers become addicted they are unable to give moral teaching to their sons, and when the master is addicted he cannot control the slave as he ought. Gambling is a cause of fights, a source of lawsuits, a reason for the rise in banditry, and a centre of attraction for the disaffected, damaging in countless ways the good morals and customs of the people .... For years now edicts have repeatedly been sent down strictly forbidding gambling, but the practice has not stopped, nor have makers of gambling equipment ceased to exist, or those who are responsible for the prohibition employed their full energies in the task .... We consider that the reason why gambling proliferates is that when fathers and elder brothers indulge in it, their sons and younger brothers take notice and emulate them; when masters indulge, their slaves and servants observe and copy them; and even women and young girls fall into the slough and do not think it blameworthy: and because so many are addicted many more become corrupted. If the prohibition were strictly enforced, no one would dare to go on infringing the law, and in course of time young men would not take up the habit; and if no one were acquiring the habit, then it would of course die out and there would be no necessity for further orders of this kind .... From now on when gamblers are apprehended there must be a careful examination of their equipment to see where it was made, and when there is clear evidence of the county of origin of the equipment the county magistrate of that place shall be dismissed for dereliction of duty, the prefectural magistrate shall be deprived of title but allowed to remain in office, and all their superior officers in the province shall be demoted one grade but allowed to remain in office. If a county magistrate manages to discover and bring to justice someone manufacturing gambling equipment in his own territory he shall be promoted two grades, his prefectural magistrate shall be promoted one grade, and their provincial superiors shall each receive a double record of merit entry. This scheme of reward and punishment shall be permanent and shall commence in AD 1730. The provincial authorities shall ensure that even in the remotest corners of town and country everyone shall be aware of it.

T.7

The Coastal guards (AD 1729)
諭沿海弁兵

p.37

Guangdong Province has the sea on three sides and a very large number of merchants from all over China as well as foreign barbarians[4] are constantly voyaging to and fro with their goods for trade. The sea winds are unpredictable and if merchant ships are wrecked it is up to the coastal guards to do all they can to save the lives of the men and to salvage the goods which are floating around in the water. The purpose of setting up the national coastal guard was not just to catch bandits and pirates. But now whenever there is a wreck unscrupulous guards greedy for gain make the most of their opportunities for pillage and they totally neglect their duty to save lives. With such behaviour they are unquestionably more shameful and utterly evil than the bandits or pirates themselves. How could soldiers of the state bear to act like this?

In September-October 1728, for instance, while returning from a trading voyage to the west, Xu Bang, a merchant of Longxi County, Fujian Province ran into a storm off the coast of Xinning County, Guangdong Province and his ship was lost. A patrol led by Captain Deng Cheng[5] of the Guangdong Coastal Garrison salvaged all the money and divided it among themselves meanwhile looking on impassively at Xu Bang and his crew without doing anything to rescue them from their danger. This case is now being investigated and a trial is pending.

Again in December 1728-January 1729 a barbarian ship from Macau in Xiangshan County returning home after the trading season was wrecked in a storm at Huitong County, Qiongzhou Prefecture. Sergeant Wen Xiu from the local fort went out immediately in a small boat and ferried off all the goods. But when he had got them ashore he only handed over a few bolts of satin and some silver utensils to the owner — the rest he hid away and would not give up. The local officials now have the matter under investigation. This kind of vicious, illegal behaviour is commonplace in Guangdong and Fujian, and is not unknown along the river banks and shores of other provinces.

Since the senior officials fail to give proper guidance in normal times and are even less capable of carrying out an investigation and taking disciplinary action when such things happen, the unscrupulous soldiery are encouraged to think only of selfish gain and not to care about saving life.

From now on if this kind of things occurs it will be severely dealt with under the statute of augmented punishment so as to act as a deterrent to the guards. When the viceroys and governors of coastal provinces have put forward their own ideas on this in memorials to the throne, the Nine Ministers in council will also deliberate on it and after promulgation the edict shall be at once communicated to the guards and also shall be subject to further consideration and memorials.

T.8

Order to issue grain loans (AD 1738)
令出借常平穀

p.51

In July-August 1736 We issued a decree that loans of grain from the public granaries should be made available to the people everywhere. The regulation that interest should be added when the loan is returned should only be enforced when it is a normal matter of the grain's being borrowed in the spring to tide people over till harvest. But when there has been a bad harvest it is a different matter; then the borrowers should only have to pay back in the autumn the amount they borrowed, and no interest should be added. This applies to state run and locally run granaries alike. Now We are informed that in some provinces loans from granaries are not made according to this general rule and people who borrow grain after a bad harvest are still required to return it with interest. This is not in the spirit of Our decree. From now on any people who borrow grain in years of poor harvest (whether from state or community granaries) are to repay it after the autumn entirely interest-free. So may all receive Our bounty. This regulation is to apply permanently.

T.9

Exemption of importing vessels from grain tax (AD 1743)
諭免外洋商船米税

p.52

We are ever mindful of the hardships of Our people, and as rice is their staple food, tax on it is to be remitted at all customs posts, while taxes on other goods will be levied according to the regulations. Foreign merchants shipping rice into the interior should be shown special favour as a mark of Our compassion for those who come from afar. In September-October 1742 some Siamese merchants brought rice to Fujian Province, and We decreed the waiving of the relevant shipped goods taxes. We understand that this year they have come again to sell their rice in Fujian and their repeated visits must be the result of favour shown them. From this year on the standing regulation will be that if a foreign ship comes to Fujian, Guangdong or other coastal province bearing more than 10,000 *dan* of rice, 50 per cent of the shipped goods tax shall be remitted; and if it carries between 5,000 and 10,000 *dan* 30 per cent of the tax shall be remitted. The rice shall then be offered for sale at the market price. If the people already have enough rice and do not buy it, then let the officials buy it either to replenish the various granaries or to distribute it as military rations to the coastal garrisons. In order that the foreign merchants shall be able to trade profitably and without trouble let the Ministry immediately issue a notice to this effect to the concerned viceroys, governors and military commanders, and let this edict be transmitted to the rulers of the foreign countries for information.

T.10

Table of the county's administrative history
沿革表

p.66

Period	Administration	Translator's notes
In the days of Yao and Shun	Nan Jiao	Mythical rulers. According to Qu Dajun, *Guangdong xinyu*, p.30, Nan Jiao was the same as Yue 粵, the ancient name for south China.
Three Dynasties	Southern Yangzhou	The three dynasties were Xia (1989-1559 BC?) Shang (1558-1051 BC?) and Zhou (1050-222 BC)
Qin	Panyu District of Nanhai Department	221-207 BC
Han	Boluo County	206 BC – AD 219
Three Kingdoms	Boluo County	AD 220-264
Jin	Bao'an District of Dongguan Department	AD 265-419
Song	Bao'an County of Dongguan Department	AD 420-478
Qi	Bao'an County of Dongguan Department	AD 479-501

Period	Administration	Translator's notes
Liang	Bao'an County. In the period 502-519 the name Dongguan 東官 was changed to Dongguan 東莞 but Bao'an was unaffected	AD 502-556
Chen	Bao'an County of Dongguan Department	AD 557-588
Sui	Bao'an County of Guangzhou. In 589 Dongguan was abolished and the county was given to Guangzhou. Then in 607 Guangzhou Prefecture was abolished and the county came under Nanhai Department	AD 589-617
Tang	Dongguan County. In 757 it came under the jurisdiction of Guangzhou Prefecture	AD 618-906
Five Dynasties	Donguan County of Xingwang Prefecture	AD 907-959
Song	Dongguan County of Guangzhou Prefecture	AD 960-1279
Yuan	Dongguan County of Guangzhou Division	AD 1280-1367
Ming	Xin'an County. In 1573 it was created from the Dongguan County frontier guard area, and put under the control of Guangzhou Prefecture	AD 1368-1643
Qing	As previous. In 1666 it was abolished and became part of Dongguan County, but was reinstated in 1669.	AD 1644-(1911)

T.11

Boundaries
疆域

p.73

The county measures 270 *li*[6] by 380 *li*. (The old edition of this gazetteer erroneously gives these as '90 *li* by more than 100 *li*'.) East of the county seat it stretches 220 *li* to the Sanguanbi Sea where it meets the border of Bijia District of Guixin County. (Old edition: 'eastward 80 *li* to Hantang'ao'.) To the west it is 50 *li* to the Fanshi Sea where it meets the border of Qi'ao District of Xiangshan County. (Old edition: 'westward 10 *li* to Xiangshan County'.) To the south it is 300 *li* to the Dan'ganshan Sea, beyond which are the unbounded deeps of the Black Water Ocean. (The old boundary is wrongly given as Fotangmen.) To the north it stretches 80 *li* to Yang'ao Shan where it meets the border of Quekou District of Dongguan County. (Old edition: 'north 60 *li* to Lianhuafeng' which is wrong. In any case Lianhuafeng is more to the north-west, not due north.)

To the north-east it is 150 *li* to Xixiang'ao Shan where it meets Bijia District of Guixin County. (Old edition: 'north-east 90 *li* to Yang'ao Shan'.) To the south-west it is 120 *li* to Sanya Shan where lies the border with the Macao Territory of Xiangshan County. (Old edition: 'south-west to Xiangshan Fort'.) To the north-west it is 80 *li* to the Helan Sea where it meets the border of Quekou District of Dongguan County. (Old edition: 'north-west to Hutoumen'.) To the south-east it is 240 *li* to Tuoning Shan on the border of Bijia District of Guixin County. (Old edition: 'south-east 150 *li* to Pinghai Guard-post by land'.)

Xin'an is different topographically from other coastal areas. Other places have the coast as their boundary, but Xin'an has many outlying islands and these are all inhabited. For this reason it is necessary to include the sea in the reckoning, otherwise the island population would be left out. A county's jurisdiction is determined by its territory, not vice versa, so the sea must be counted in. The old gazetteer dealt only with the mainland area under the county's control, thus making all its figures unreliable. Just to take the southern boundary as an example: the old gazetteer says that it is Fotangmen; but are the people who live beyond Fotangmen on islands like Putai, Changzhou, Dayu Shan and Dan'gan Shan not to be entered on the population registers of Xin'an? The prefectural gazetteer also states that Xin'an extends 40 *li* to the sea, but it is wrong even in saying that it is 40 *li* from the county seat to the sea. Now the combined area of land and sea is counted in the reckoning right out to the furthest island.

Again, the lie of the county is long towards the east and short to the west, it is broad in the south-east and narrow in the north-west, because the county seat is off-centre in the north-west. The map of the county in the old gazetteer placed the county seat in the middle, and so got the directions wrong. Now nearly all these have been corrected and the area is properly drawn and the boundaries are accurate.

The county seat is 240 *li* from the prefectural city and over 8,000 *li* from the capital.[7]

T.12

Wind-lore
風異

p.76

In the 6th, 7th and 8th months there are typhoons 颶風. They are presaged by broken rainbows. Still clouds build up thickly, there is continuous rumbling thunder, the sea seethes, the water pounds on the rocks with great noise, and sea-birds fly panic-stricken before the wild gusts. Often a north wind blows all night long, houses are blown down, crops ruined, trees uprooted and boats sunk. The typhoon only finishes when the winds change from easterly to westerly and then southerly — this is called 'returning south'. If they fail to 'return south' then the typhoon comes back two days later. There is a popular saying: 'If Mother Typhoon does not return south then in less than three days she will reappear, either to blow furiously for a short while (a few hours or a day and a night) or less violently but for a longer time (perhaps two or three days).'

T.13

Customs
風俗

p.80

The populace is primarily concerned with agriculture and silk-making[8] and very little involved in commerce. There are two harvests a year. Their farm tools are strongly-made and the people are straightforward in their dealings.

Formerly most houses had mud walls, the barest protection from wind and rain, but now they are built with plaster and good blue bricks.[9]

Great care is taken to select marriage partners of the appropriate social status, and not even the poorest families will intermarry with 'mean people'.[10]

The old-established lineages of the county have lands set aside for the financing of ancestor worship ceremonies, which are performed once or twice every year. They also provide money for the support of their young men who are licentiates, paper and books for those taking local examinations and travelling expenses for those going off to the provincial examinations. In famine years the lineages distribute relief in the form of money or grain to their poorer members. If any member breaks the lineage rules or allows himself to become a slave he is banned from membership of the lineage in accordance with ancient practice.

On marriage there is a custom called 'passing gifts' where presents of betel-nut, artemisia leaves and ceremonial buns are made. The groom does not go to meet his bride in person — they first meet in a temple on the evening of the wedding day.

When a family is marrying out a daughter it does not make a great display of dowry, but sends candied plums to friends and relations as an invitation to the wedding feast, the custom being known simply as 'sending the candied plums', while the feast is called the 'plum banquet'.

The people patronize shamans and believe in spirits. If someone is ill they get an old woman to dress in mourning clothes and stand at the door burning incense and chanting prayers, or else they invite a Taoist priest to exorcize the evil spirits with blasts of his horn all night long. They have a saying that when the grain is ripe the ghosts will appear. Ghosts come looking for food, but can be exorcized with fire.

They consider old age to start at 61, placing emphasis on the decades plus one, rather than round tens ....

On the day before the beginning of Spring the God Mangshen, who is the herd of the Earth Ox, is welcomed down at the foot of Nan Shan. On the next morning he 'whips in the Spring'. On this day the people worship in their ancestral halls. On the 15th day of the new year they celebrate with lanterns and music, and anyone who has had a son born in the previous year lights an auspicious lantern. The fourth day after that is popularly known as 'Heaven's clothes day' and the people make special cakes decorated on the top with needle and thread. These are offered in sacrifice to Heaven in a ceremony called 'Mending Heaven's clothes'. On the 14th day of the 7th lunar month and on the Winter Solstice they sacrifice ducks in worship of their ancestors. they sweep their ancestral graves at Chongyang[11] in the same way as at Qingming.[12] Other festivals are mostly the same as those in the *Jingchusuishiji* 荊楚歲時記.[13]

The county is bounded by the sea and many of the people fish for their livelihood. The farmers are hard-working but their lands adjoin those of Dongguan and Guishan counties whose peoples migrate in to live amongst ours. Sometimes the farmers' fields are too far off to farm themselves and then they are occupied by the tenants so that they have to be sold off at a low price. Thus their livelihood depends on those in authority supporting the weak against the strong: and this should be noted.

T.14

Villages
都里

p.119

According to the old gazetteer the county was divided into 3 *Xiang*, 7 *Dou*, 57 *Tu*, and nearly 500 *Cun*. But upon investigation it can be seen that there are muddles and errors in most of the *Dou* lists, and only six or seven out of ten are the same in both editions. In the 7th *Dou* dozens of villages in the Changshantou/Shitanpu/Lincun/Lianhu area are still under Dongguan County, while more than ten villages including Dunjiaozi, Toujianxiang and Weiyang'ao have now fallen into ruins. The different names in the two gazetteers also make precise comparison difficult. But we can now see that there are over 570 Punti villages and more than 270 Hakka settlements. They are divided into administrative areas under the Deputy Magistrate, the Chief of Police, and the two Assistant Magistrates, each village being listed separately and the Hakka lists appended. Thus all entries are orderly and there can be no problem about finding them under their correct listing.

T.15

Mountains
山

p.141

Wutong Mountain lies 60 *li* to the east of the county seat. It has three fine peaks and measures several score *li* around. On the north side it runs down to the Eastern Sea, and on the south it forms the border of the county.[14] At the top there is the fathomless Heavenly Pool, with many wutong trees and rare plants, and at the foot is Red Water Cave. The mountain is the dragon on which the county geomantically depends.

Yangtai Mountain is 30 *li* north of the county seat. Lofty and verdant it has at the top Dragon Pool where prayers for rain are straightway answered, and at the bottom Peaceful Garden Monastery. It is a spur of Wutong Mountain and the county seat relies on it geomantically.

Wengang Hill is about 3 *li* north-east of the county seat. Also known as Jiangang Hill, it is 40 *zhang* high and 200 *zhang* around. It is an outlier of Yangtai Mountain.

Nan Shan is on the sea coast 7 *li* from the county seat. On top of it are Twin

Stone Pagoda and Guanyin Hall, and there is a stone like an immortal's foot where the local people pray for rain ....

p. 145

Guijiao Hill is 40 *li* south-east of the county seat. Cassia trees grow profusely there. There are two hills which vie for the honour of being the most beautiful horn-shape: the other is called Aotan Hill. This one, whenever it has cloud on it, it is bound to rain. On top is a rock called 'Immortal Maiden at her Toilet'. In the Song dynasty Deng Fu built the Liying School at the foot of the hill, and the foundations can still be seen there today.

Meiwei Hill is 100 *li* south of the county seat. It acts both as defence for the city and as a barrier against the Eastern Sea. It is thickly wooded, and the Song dynasty emperor Jingyan established his travelling palace there.

Guanfu Hill is east of Jishuimen and this side of Fotangmen. The Song emperor Jingyan's floating court arrived here and the remains of his palace are still to be seen. Formerly there was an assistant magistracy here, but now it has moved to Chiwei Village.

Daxi Shan, otherwise known as Dayu Shan [Lantau], is more than 100 *li* south of the county seat and separates Jishuimen from Fotangmen. There are thirty-six peaks on the island, which has a circumference of over 200 *li*. If rare birds are seen there, it presages a typhoon. On the island many villages are involved in salt-pan working. In the Song dynasty the island was granted to Li Wenjian, and the Li family still has it.

T.16

Waters
水

p.151

Du'ao Sea is 200 *li* south of the county seat. To the left of it is Fotangmen, and to the right is Jishuimen.

Jishuimen is south of Guanfu Hill.

Liyumen is to the south of Guanfu Hill.

Fotangmen is south-east of Liyumen. It is also known as Anvil Narrows because beside it is a great rock more than 2 *zhang* long shaped like an anvil. When the tide rips through, great waves fling themselves to heaven, and if the winds are not with them merchant vessels dare not try the passage. The north part is called North Fotang and the south is South Fotang. At either end is a Tianhou Temple. The one at the north end has a carved stone inscription from the Song dynasty, with several columns of characters each as big as a rice bowl. They have been there a long time and have become obliterated, but the four characters 咸淳二年 [AD 1266] can be made out still. To the right of the temple is Anchor Fluke Bay, where there used to be a customs post. The foundations remain. To the south is Fotang's hill, an isolated island. In the Kangxi reign [1662-1722] a fort was built on it as an anti-pirate measure, but in 1810 County Magistrate Li Weiyu petitioned to have the fort resited on the coast at Kowloon Commandery.[15]

T.17

Civil establishment
文官制

p.161

1 County Magistrate
- 7 Document clerks
- 1 Sorting clerk
- 1 Granary clerk
- 1 Treasury clerk[16]

1 Deputy Magistrate for Dapeng (established in 1723)
- 1 General clerk

EDUCATION

1 Director of Studies (abolished in 1664 and re-established in 1678)

1 Assistant Director of Studies
- 1 General clerk

1 Assistant Magistrate for Guanfu District
- 1 General clerk

1 Assistant Magistrate for Fuyong District
- 1 General clerk

1 Chief of Police[17]
- 1 General clerk

1 Supervisor of the Dongguan Chang (abolished in 1789)
- 1 Collecting clerk (abolished)

1 Supervisor of the Gui'de Chang (abolished in 1789)
- 1 Collecting clerk (abolished)

(According to the old gazetteer, in the Ming dynasty there were two Granary Supervisors (for the Dapeng and Yongying granaries) and one Collecting Officer, but the posts have long since been abolished.)

T.18

Walled and moated cities

城池

p.241

The county seat was built on Chengzi Hill on the site of the old Dongguan Guard-post. The city was started in AD 1394 by Cui Hao, the Guangzhou Lieutenant of the Left Guard. Including subsidiary walls there is a total length of wall of 578 *zhang* 5 *chi.*[18] It is 2 *zhang* high and tapers from 2 *zhang* thick at the base to 1 *zhang* at the top. There are four gates: the east gate is called Jukui Gate, the west is Jenhai Gate, the south is Ning Gate, the outer south gate is Ying'en Gate, and the north is Gongchen Gate. The county was created in AD 1573. (According to the old gazetteer it was built in 1570, but the 'Geography' section of the official *Ming Dynasty History* says: 'Xin'an County is under Guangzhou Prefecture. It was created from the Dongguan Guard-post area in 1573.' We amend here to the latter date). County Magistrate Wu Daxun[19] claimed that the north gate was on the backbone of the county and that it was not fitting for it to be opened right over the dragon's vein which ran up to it,[20] so he had it blocked up and only the east, west and south gates used. There were four gate-towers and four watch-towers, twenty-five guard stations, 1,200 parapet embrasures, three drawbridges, and two sluice-gates, one at the south-east corner and one at the south-west. In 1577 Magistrate Zeng Kongzhi added subsidiary walls at the east, west and south gates, and also three gate-towers and four watch-towers....

Dapeng City is situated at the foot of Dapeng Ridge, 160 *li* from the county seat. (The old gazetteer erroneously states 120 *li*.) It was begun in 1394 by the Guangzhou Lieutenant of the Left Guard Zhang Bin. Faced on the outside and inside with brick and stone the wall has a circumference of 327 *zhang* 6 *chi*. It is 1 *zhang* 8 *chi* high, 6 *chi* thick at the top and 1 *zhang* 4 *chi* at the bottom. There are four gate-towers and four watch-towers, sixteen guard stations, and 654 parapet embrasures. There is water on three sides of it to a length of 398 *zhang*, and it is 1 *zhang* 5 *chi* wide by 1 *zhang* deep....

The Deputy Magistrate's yamen is in Dapeng.

The Guanfu Assistant Magistrate's yamen is at Chiwei Village, thirty or so *li* from the county seat. The original yamen was 80 *li* to the south-east of the county seat and served Guanfu Commandery. In 1370 it was made an Assistant Magistracy at the same time as Fuyong. The yamen buildings were dilapidated for a long while and those who came to take up post there had to rent houses from the inhabitants. In 1671 the Assistant Magistrate Jiang Zhenyuan donated money from his salary to buy land from the Chiwei villagers and to build the present yamen.

The Fuyong Assistant Magistrate's yamen is south of Fuyong Village, 30 *li* from the county seat. It was originally the Tunmen/Guxu Commandery, but it was made an Assistant Magistracy in 1370 and housed in two buildings. In 1664 with the coastal removal they were demolished, to be rebuilt in 1671 by Assistant Magistrate Xue Zhen.

T.19

Military offices
武署

p.249

The Major's Offices were on the right-hand side of the Dongguan Guard-post and next to the Naval Commander's Offices in Yongying Street in the county city. They were built in 1595 by Acting Lieutenant-Colonel Major Qin Jingguo as the Lieutenant-Colonel's Offices. In 1650 they collapsed from long exposure to the elements, and all the garrison were billeted in the homes of the population. In 1669 Major Yin Zhen donated money with which the offices were rebuilt exactly as they had been before, and he added archery butts and an 'Honour the Best' pavilion. But in 1671 a typhoon demolished them. Major Cai Chang repaired the damage, but in 1686 a typhoon again wrecked them. Major Lin Rui repaired them but later they again became derelict. Now the Major occupies the same offices as the Second Captain in Ying'en Street.

The Second Captain's Offices were in Yongying Street next to the Naval Commander's Offices, but they have long been derelict and he now lives in Ying'en Street.

The Dapeng Lieutenant-Colonel's Offices are inside Dapeng City.

The Dapeng Second Captain's Offices are inside Dapeng City.

T.20

The school
學校

p.251

The school-temple is sited on Wengang Hill beyond the east gate of the city and facing Beidu. It was built in 1573 by County Magistrate Wu Daxun and Director of Studies Yu Xiang. By 1595 the buildings were derelict, and County

Magistrate Yu Zhu, Director of Studies Shi Kongjian[21] and Assistant Director of Studies Sun Guangzuo rebuilt it to the left of the Coastal Defence Station south of the city. Their work was completed by County Magistrate Li Ruxiang.[22] In 1642 County Magistrate Zhou Xiyao decided that the poor results in the civil service examinations were caused by the school-temple's geomantic position, and he subscribed money towards resiting it once more outside the east gate. In 1671 it was demolished by a typhoon. County Magistrate Li Kecheng proposed to restore it, but in 1676 before it was done pirates came pillaging and not a stone was left standing. In 1679 County Magistrate Zhang Mingda set aside a sum for rebuilding and when Director of Studies Huang Gunshang took office the following year[23] he energetically gave assistance so that the project was finished in 1682. In 1782 County Magistrate Wu Yi set about restoring the building, and the work was completed under County Magistrate Li Dagen in 1784.

As it stands now there is the Main Hall of Confucius in the centre, and in front of it a terrace protected by a stone balustrade. There are ceremonial corridors leading out from the east and west corners to fine gates. To the east is the Hall of Celebrated Officials and to the west the Hall of Local Worthies. The two Official Pavilions face each other on the left and right. To the south is a semicircular pool crossed by a stone bridge, and beyond that is an ornamental arch made entirely of stone. Behind the main hall is the Hall of Exalted Sages and behind that again the Repository of the Classics, on the east of which is the Hall of Filial and Fraternal Piety, and on the west the Hall of Loyalty and Righteousness. To the left of the main hall is the Hall of High Principles with the Promotion of Virtue Library and the Cultivation of Scholarship Library behind, and beyond them the Pavilion of the God of Literature. At the south-east corner of the pavilion is the Earth God shrine. To the right of the main hall is the Hall of Guandi,[24] at the back of which is the Hall of the Three Ancient Dynasties, with the quarters for the school gatekeepers to the west of it. Surrounding all is a red wall outside of which on the south is a stone balustrade and then a pond. Everything is on a magnificent and imposing scale.[25]

T.21

Temples
壇廟

p.253

The Shrine to the Gods of Soil and Grain 社稷壇 is outside the city wall at the south-west corner. It was built in 1573 by the County Magistrate Wu Daxun. It is twenty feet wide, by twenty feet deep, and rises in two steps to a height of more than two feet. The shrine is surrounded by a wall with gates which are opened and shut at the appropriate times. It is north-facing and entry is made by the north gate when worshipping. The tablets of the gods are made of wood, 2½ feet high, 4½ inches wide and 1 inch thick, set in a base 4½ inches high by 8½ inches wide and 4½ inches thick. The names of the gods are written on them: one says 'God of the County's Soil' and the other 'God of the County's Grain'. Both tablets have gold writing on red lacquer. The Soil God is placed on the west of the altar and the Grain God on the east. When not being worshipped they are stored away.

p.255

The Hall of Celebrated Officials 名宦祠 is outside the east gate of the city, to the east of the Temple for Civil Rites. In it are worshipped seventeen officials: from the Ming dynasty there are the Secretary to the Board of War, Wang Hong; the Circuit Intendent, Liu Wen; the Coastal Defence Sub-prefect, Zhou Xiyin; County Magistrates, Wu Daxun, Yu Zhu and Qiu Tiqian; Director of Studies, Shi Kongjian; and Assistant Director of Studies, Sun Guangzuo; while from the present dynasty there are the Viceroy of Guangdong and Guangxi, Kong Yuxun; Governor of Guangdong, Yang Zongren; Viceroy, Zhou Youde; Governors, Wang Lairen, Yang Wenqian and Zhu Hongzuo; and County Magistrates, Jin Qizhen, Ding Tangfa and Tang Ruoshi.

p.257

The Governor Wang Halls 王巡撫祠 are for worshipping Wang Lairen who was Governor of Guangdong Province. There is one in Xixiang, one in Shatou Market, and one in Shihu Market. Governor Wang petitioned the throne for permission to repopulate the evacuated territory. (See 'Memorials' section.)

T.22

Population
户口

p.269

	Year	*Households*	*Persons*	*Males*	*Females*
Ming	1573	7608	33971	—	—
Dynasty	1582	7752	34520	19627	14883[26]
	1593	7752	13202	—	—
	1603	3572	16675	—	—
	1613	3500	16696	—	—
	1622	3500	16248	—	—
	1632	3491	16992	—	—

	Year	*Households*	*Persons*	*Males*	*Females*
	1642	3589	17871	—	—
Qing Dynasty	16 (44-61)[27]	2966	6851	5567	1284
	1662 & 1664	after 2 evacuations there still remained	—	2172	—
	1667	—	—	2255	1412
	1672	—	3972	—	—
	1669-1671	—	—	1648 returned from evacuation. 1501 assessable for salt tax.	
	1673-1685	—	4525	957 returned from evacuation, and were newly added to the register. 1585 assessable for salt tax.	
	1686-1711	new registrations were	—	303	359
	1713	by imperial decree no liability for tax on any future increase in population by birth	—	—	—
	1716 1721 1726	new registrations graciously exempted from tax	—	11	—
	1731	newly registered returnees	—	5	—
	1686-1731	original assessment plus new registrations exempt from tax and all new registrations	7289	—	—
		made up of	—	5332	1284
		+exempt new registrations	—	11	—
		+new registrations	—	303	359
	1736-1761	a prosperous age with many new births registered	—	2855	—
		(assessable for salt tax)	—	(730)	—

Year	*Households*	*Persons*	*Males*	*Females*
1741-1761	a reduction of	—	208	—
	(salt tax quota)	—	(10)	—
1766	a reduction of	—	75	—
	The actual increase by birth was:	—	2572	—
	(salt tax quota)	—	(720)	—
	and it was graciously decreed that there should be no further tax quota increases			
1766	a prosperous age: new registrations	—	407	—
1771	a reduction of	—	88	—
	the actual increase by birth was	—	319	—
	it was graciously decreed that there should be no further tax quota increase			
1771	a prosperous age: new registrations	—	402	—
	it was graciously decreed that there should be no further tax quota increase			
	Incorporated on the closing of the Dong-guan Garrison		46.8[28]	
1772	from this year the practice of registering numbers of new births ceased. They were no longer entered in the main books but in separate annual reports[29]			
1772	The first such report:			
	civilians & salt-workers	30373	21121	9252
	garrison personnel	1821	1356	465

Year	*Households*	*Persons*	*Males*	*Females*
1773-1818	Discounting deletions the actual number of new births plus those originally reported was:			
	civilians & salt-workers	225979	146922	79057
	garrison personnel	13136	8298	4838

T.23

Land-tax
田賦

p.273

The 'original quota' of padi land, dry land, hill land, ponds, marine land, and valley land held by officials, common people, salt-workers, priests, etc., in 1573 was 2911 *qing* 47 *mu* 2 *fen* 5 *li* 5 *hao*....

The 'operating quota' which our dynasty has determined shall remain is:

Padi land: 3760 *qing* 33 *mu* 3 *fen* 1 *li* 4 *hao*
Dry land: 236 *qing* 43 *mu* 1 *fen* 1 *li* 8 *hao*
Valley land: 1 *qing* 56 *mu* 2 *fen* 6 *li* 4 *hao*
Ponds: 26 *qing* 98 *mu* 3 *fen* 8 *li*
Lakes: 63 *mu* 8 *fen* 7 *li* 7 *hao*
Marine land: 48 *mu* 4 *fen* 8 *li* 4 *hao*
Sand bars: 61 *mu* 7 *fen* 1 *li* 5 *hao*
Reservoirs: 1 *mu* 5 *fen*
Streams: 2 *mu* 2 *fen*
Brooks: 2 *fen*
Hill land: 12 *qing* 47 *mu* 7 *fen* 1 *li* 3 *hao*

The tax liability for the above totals 4,039 *qing* 56 *mu* 7 *fen* 6 *li* 5 *hao* 6 *si*.

T.24

The Xiangyin Banquet
鄉飲酒禮

p.297

The ceremony is held in the Hall of High Principles[30] every year on the 15th of the 1st month and the 1st of the 10th month. The senior official of the prefecture or county acts as host, retired officials act as assistant hosts, and selected local worthies of advanced age are secondary guests, being seated in order of seniority. The host sits in the south-east, with the chief guests in the north-west, assistant hosts in the north-east and secondary guests in the south-west. Scholars attached to the academy sit in the west in order of rank and facing the commoner guests who sit in the east in order of age. The County Education Officer acts as Master of Ceremonies....

The operating quotas for the *Xiangyin* banquet are: one retired official as Chief Guest, one elderly scholar as Secondary Guest, one elderly commoner as Elderly Guest. The Assistant Host's place is taken by the Education Officer and elderly guests take the Commoner Guests places.....

T.25

Hakka examination quotas
客籍學額

p.308

At the *sui* examinations —	civil	2 places
	military	2 places
At the *ke* examinations —	civil	2 places

Following the reoccupation of the evacuated territory there was more land than people, and a decree was issued encouraging the opening up of military lands. Hakka people from Jiangxi and Fujian as well as from the Huizhou/Chaozhou/Jiaying region of Guangdong came pouring into Xin'an and took up the military land. In 1716 they were entered in the military establishment and assigned a pass quota of two places in each of the civil and military examinations. In 1735 this was abolished and merged with the military quota. In 1802 an Imperial decree established a separate Hakka examination quota, with two places in each of the civil and military examinations at the *sui* examination and two places in the *ke* civil examination.[31]

T.26

The Fenggang Academy
鳳岡書院

p.311

The Fenggang Academy is situated in Heyang Street in the southern part of the city. It was originally the site of the Coastal Defence Office, but in 1679 it became the Dongguan Centre Salt Office. In 1801 came the order to abolish the Dongguan Centre. The buildings were converted into an academy under the successive hands of magistrates Sun Shuxin, Wang Tingjin, Zhu Linzheng and

Xu Sun,[32] and Provincial Treasurer Kang Jitian honoured the academy by writing the name board 'Fenggang Academy'. In the centre is the lecture hall opening onto a terrace with the main approach below it. On its left is the east library and on its right the west. To the front is the main gate with two ancient banyan trees just outside, then the wall, and beyond that the entrance gate and two small lodges for the gatekeepers. Behind the lecture hall is the Hall of Former Sages, and behind that again is the Kuixing Tower.[33] (Provincial Grain Intendant Zhang Quan wrote the board in it bearing the words 'Listening to Rain Gallery'). On either side is built a decorative pavilion with eight study rooms ranged to left and right and some spare land behind. There is a wall all round. A local man Liu Zhuanghua and others made endowments of land, and County Magistrate Xu Sun wrote the regulations for behaviour and had them inscribed on a tablet and set up in the academy beside the Hall of Former Sages. (See the 'Literary Excerpts' section for the text of the tablet.[34])

T.27

Public lectures
宣講

p.316

The Sacred Edict will be read on the 1st and 15th days of every month at the large, clean public place selected for it. Civil and military officials shall attend in ceremonial dress. The Master of Ceremonies shall call out the order of events and the ceremony of three kneelings and nine kotows shall be performed, after which all shall repair to the lecture spot where the soldiery and populace shall gather around in orderly and respectful fashion to hear the Master of Ceremonies call for the lecture to commence. The lecturer and the Master of Ceremonies shall kneel in front of the incense table and hold up the Sacred Edict, then ascend the rostrum and toll the signal bell. A venerable person shall kneel and read the Edict aloud, and then the Master of Ceremonies shall invite the lecturer to expound the first clause of the Edict, and so on clause by clause. When finished, the ceremony is over.

T.28

Saving the sun
救護

p.316

Before a solar eclipse an incense table shall be set up on the terrace of the

County Magistracy, a golden drum shall be placed at the Ceremonial Gate, musicians shall stand below the terrace, and the worshippers on the terrace itself. All shall face the sun, and when the time arrives and the *Yinyang* Professor reports the beginning of the eclipse, all the officials (civil and military alike) shall chant in praise of the sun and perform the three kneelings and nine kotows. Then the senior official shall beat the drum three times and the rest of the drums shall start to sound, stopping only when it is reported that the sun is fully restored to its round shape. The officials shall again perform three kneelings and nine kotows and that ends the proceedings. A similar ceremony is held for a lunar eclipse.

T.29

Taking up office
涖任

p.318

On the first day of a new posting [the County Magistrate] should go to the City God Temple 城隍廟 to observe a fast. He should sacrifice to the god early next morning, and then go to the ceremonial gate of the yamen to make sacrifice. After these rites he should dress in full ceremonial robes, face north-east and express his gratitude for the imperial bounty extended to him. Then he should change out of ceremonial dress and receive courtesy callers. Three days after his arrival he should go to the school-temple to make offerings.

Every month on the 1st and 15th days he should go to worship first at the Temple for Civil Rites, then at the City God Temple, then at the Temple of the Empress of Heaven 天后廟 and finally at the Earth God Shrine 土地祠 .[35]

T.30

Military establishment
兵制

p.347

At the beginning of the Ming Hongwu reign[36] the emperor Zhu Liangzu pacified Guangdong and ordered the Regional Commanders to set up garrisons and guards at strategic locations. In 1384 Commander Hua Mao memorialized that additional posts should be set up along the coast with beacons built and military farm settlements established where the troops could support themselves by agriculture when not engaged in defence against the Japanese pirates. The military system was very elaborate....

The Qing Shunzhi Emperor established a Xin'an defence force with a complement of one captain, one lieutenant and two sergeants. In 1664 a major was added to the strength, the captain became adjutant-captain and there was a quota of two patrol lieutenants (of the left and right) and four patrol sergeants (left and right). In 1665 a Brigadier-General was posted in, but transferred again in 1668....

At present the Xin'an Battalion has one major, one adjutant-captain, two patrol lieutenants, four patrol sergeants, and five corporals (all of them stationed at the county seat).

Originally the strength of the battalion was 500 men, but when the border was changed in 1664 it was increased by 500. It was reduced to 708 men in 1682....

The present establishment with the 5 corporals is exactly 1,000 men (including 20 cavalry men, 293 infantrymen, and 682 patrol guards). There are 25 war horses.

The annual pay of the whole battalion, officers and men is 13,946 taels 4.74 cash, plus 3,642.91 *dan* of rice and 15,182 bundles of hay.....

p.351

Dapeng Guard Battalion (大鵬所防守營). This was originally formed with one lieutenant in the early years of the Qing Shunzhi Emperor. In 1656 the force was strengthened by the addition of a captain, a lieutenant and two sergeants....Now the battalion is offered by a lieutenant-colonel, an adjutant-captain, two patrol lieutenants, four patrol sergeants and seven corporals (all stationed at Dapeng). The complement of other ranks was originally 300, but 200 more came in to bring the numbers up to 500 in 1656. In 1704 more men were brought in to establish a marine corps, and there are now 800 altogether, made up of 190 infantry and 610 patrol guards. The seven corporals and seven supplymen are not included in these figures.

The officers of the battalion draw a total annual pay of 574 taels 0.46 cash, and the men, corporals and supplymen draw 10,866 taels. In addition they draw 3,096 *dan* of rice and 8,640 bundles of hay.

T.31

Charities administration
卹政

p.355

There are two Charitable Institutions 養濟院. One is outside the north gate of the city on the left of the County Plague Shrine. It has an office and twenty small buildings and is a home for the blind. The other is 2 *li* beyond the east gate at the foot of the Three Rocks. It consists of one office and dozens of small buildings, and houses the insane. Both were built by the County Magistrate Wu Daxun in 1573.

There are two Charitable Gardens 漏澤園 [37] which have the duty of burying the uncared for dead in accordance with the responsibility of a benevolent government to 'cover stray bones and bury rotting flesh'.[38] One of them is beside the Guanyin Temple outside the west gate and the other outside the north gate. (This is recorded in the old gazetteer.)

There is an established fund for the support of ninety-nine people who are orphaned, aged, insane or ill. It amounts to 356 tales 4 cash, with an additional 29 taels 7 cash for *run* years.[39] The original fund was of 148 taels 5.02 cash, with 21 taels 7.8 cash extra for *run* years, but in 1738 there was an Imperial command to make available a supplementary sum of 207 taels 8.982 cash plus 7 taels 9.2 cash in *run* years, this money to be distributed in the county.

A supplementary fund for supporting ninety-five people who are orphaned, aged or insane totals 342 taels plus 28 taels 5 cash in *run* years, the money to be drawn from the provincial treasury for expenditure in the county.

T.32

Relief granaries
倉貯

p.356

The Ever Normal Granary consists of twelve storehouses sited outside the main gate of the county yamen. It is not known when it was established.

The Military Granary has six storehouses and is within the walls of the county yamen. It was built in 1732.

The Tribute Rice Granary is three storehouses at the side of the third hall within the county yamen. It was built in 1744.

The Prosperity Granary comprises six storehouses in the front of the Guanyin Pavilion in the north of the city. It was built in 1745.

The Scholarship Rice Granary is six storehouses beside the county hall. It was built in 1738.

These granaries hold a quota of 20,617 *dan* 5 *dou* 3 *sheng* of grain. They also contain the privately donated grain from charities throughout the county amounting to 267 *dan* 9 *dou* 5 *sheng*. (These donations are kept separate and managed independently.)

The Dapeng Military Granary is to the east of the Deputy Magistrate's yamen. Two storehouses were built in 1669, then six more were added in 1732 and later on three more. They are all in the charge of the Deputy Magistrate and can hold 1,700 *dan*.

The Ever-Full Granary. This was established in 1436 under the control of Dongguan County. After the creation of Xin'an County in 1573 it was moved to the left-hand side of the City God Temple. In 1642 it was abolished by County Magistrate Zhou Xiyao, and has since been derelict.

The Be Prepared Granary. This was housed inside and was abolished at the same time as the Ever-Full Granary.

The Dapeng Granary. Situated inside the walls of Dapeng city and founded at the same time as the Ever-Full Granary. In 1586 one storehouse was erected.

The 'ever normal' principle for grain has been accepted for a long while. In 1657 a proclamation went out to all prefectures and counties to establish granaries of both charitable and community types as preparation against famine. It was to be the responsibility of the circuit officials to inspect the old stocks and to see to the gathering in of new. Every year an account was to be submitted to the Board, the Board would scrutinize the volume or shortfall of grain in store, and after consideration they would memorialize the throne so that credit or blame could be apportioned.

T.33

Postal stations[40]
郵舖

p.357

Ximinting Staging Post:	at Baisha 20 *li* from the county seat. There were originally rooms for officials travelling to and fro to rest in. They were built by the Ming dynasty County Magistrate Zeng Kongzhi, but are now in ruins.
Shuanmenpu Staging Post:	the express office in Zhoujia village 40 *li* from the county seat. There used to be sleeping accommodation there, built in the Ming Zhengde period[41] by Governor Wu Tingju, but it is now in ruins.
Express Station:	on the left of the County Magistracy. Now in ruins.
Liutang Station:	10 *li* from the county seat.
Baisha Station:	This is Ximinting; 20 *li* from the county seat.
Limugang:	30 *li* from the county seat.

Zhoujia Village:	This is Shuanmenpu; 40 *li* from the county seat.
Lisonglang:	50 *li* from the county seat.

The above six stations extend northwards to Dongguan County on a road of strategic importance and are staffed by fourteen courier-soldiers.

Dayong Station:	5 *li* east from the county seat.
Yuegang Station:	40 *li* east from the county seat.
Pengkeng Station:	60 *li* east from the county seat.
Dalu Station:	80 *li* east from the county seat.
Xiagang Station:	100 *li* east from the county seat.
Dapeng Station:	120 *li* east from the county seat.

The above six stations extend eastwards to Dapeng. The road is an isolated one but there is no accommodation provided. At the six stations there were fourteen courier-soldiers, but in 1621 this complement was decreased by one and there are still only thirteen.

T.34

Coastal defences
海防略

p.359

In military administration nothing is more vital than defence of borders, and the most important borders are the sea coasts. The county seat looks out on the ocean and anyone going out to sea must pass through the straights and narrows of Jishui, Fotang, Du'ao and Lantau Island. To the east are Tunmen and Wangjing, and to the west are Aowan and Maozhou. Thus the Nantou Commandery is the outer defence of the Bocca Tigris and a strategic shield for the provincial capital. As for Dapeng it is an important garrison town for the defence of nearby Huizhou and Chaozhou....

The Nantou Commandery used to consist of six guard-posts, namely Fotangmen, Longchuanwan, Luoge, Da'ao, Langtaowan and Langbai. In 1586 Viceroy Wu and Censor Wang submitted in a memorial that Nantou was the gateway to the entire province and the place from which to control the barbarians and the dwarfs. They asked that a Brigadier-General should be posted there with his command. Barbarian ships were able to sail right into Macau, but from Macau to the provincial capital the water was shallow and unnavigable so that they had to go past Lantau Island and Nantou in order to get through the

Bocca Tigris and so into the Pearl River. This was why Nantou was to be thought of as the gateway to the province....

After the return to the evacuated coast in the Kangxi period the seas were made safe and the strategic defences were tightened up even more. Now the guard-posts and troop dispositions are quite different from before and the key defences are Jiyijiao Fort on Lantau Island, Nantou Fort, and the Left and Right Forts at Chiwan.

T.35

The fleet
寨船

p.361

In the Ming dynasty the old quota of warships under the Nantou Command was fifty-three vessels of various sizes. After 1591 it was constantly added to up to a total of 112 hulls, but in 1621 a proposal was approved to transfer to Xiangshan County thirty-three ships, being half those under the Right Wing of the Anti-Japanese Defence Command. This left seventy-nine ships. Later twelve small 'victory' fishing boats were converted into four vessels of six sweeps each, leaving a fleet of seventy-one. In 1629 it was decided to lay off the old ships and to build new ones. At that time there remained twelve large vessels (number threes and number fours), twenty-six fast ships comprising number sevens, fourteen-sweepers, twelve-sweepers and six-sweepers, and ten 'Victory' surveillance fishing boats, a total of forty-eight. Now they have all been done away with. (See old gazetteer, 'The Fleet' section.)

The original strength of the Xin'an Battalion was two white-hulled warjunks and five boats with sweeps; and not included in the quota were two sampans of different sizes and one dinghy. The fleet went out on patrol twice annually. In 1794 the Governor-General drew attention to the clumsiness of the warjunks in service and proposed to build boats on the model of the Zhejiang Province fighting ships. They are known as 'rice boats' 米艇 and come in three sizes. The Xin'an Battalion was issued with three of the large ones and two medium-sized ones. Later one patrol boat with a complement of fighting men was added, and of the original quota, the two warjunks and seven of the other boats were got rid of.

In 1794 the Dapeng Battalion was issued with five of the 'rice boats' large and medium with complements of men, and in 1816 two salvage vessels with their complements of fighting men were added. Of the boats not included in the old quota, four warjunks, five rowing boats for inland waters, and three fast patrol boats were scrapped.[42]

T.36

Natural disasters
災異

p.363

MING DYNASTY

1526 March/April:	There was a terrible thunderstorm.
1546 May/June:	A high tide caused a great flood.
1565 April/May:	A severe drought brought the price of rice up to 1 cash a *dou.*
1567 30 December:	An earthquake.
1578:	A comet was seen.
1583:	Summer and autumn, severe drought.
1596:	Severe drought, rice 1.6 cash a *dou.*
1597:	A sinister omen appeared.[43]
1603, 26 September:	An earthquake.
1605, 15 September:	An earthquake.
1618, October/November:	A comet was seen in the east.
1620, 16 July:	An earthquake.
1624, May/June:	Rice rose to a price of 1.5 cash a *dou.*
1629:	Oysters had blood in them so that the people did not dare eat them, and this year the plague claimed many lives.
1630, April/May:	A sinister omen shaped like a black dog bewitched women. After the County Magistrate Chen Gu had offered prayers to the City God the phenomenon vanished.
1631, May:	Rice rose to a price of 1.6 cash a *dou.*
1636, May/June/July:	Drought. Rice rose to 1.6 cash a *dou*, and relief grain was issued by the county to prevent starvation.
1643, 10 June:	A typhoon brought torrential rain, uprooted trees, demolished houses, and capsized many boats.

PRESENT DYNASTY

1647:	There appeared on Qianlong Mountain white

	vapour shaped like a sheep which changed into a mosquito and moved towards the west. Also the crows cawed non-stop for ten days and nights. Bandits created havoc this year.
1648:	Terrible famine. Rice cost 1 tael 2 cash and many people starved to death. Some cut up corpses for food. Men and women were sold for a *dou* of rice. There was plague, and robbery and banditry were rife. More than half the population died and there was one village in which not one person survived.
1652, 8 August:	Nine dragons flew up from Dragon Cave, passed over Chenshang and Chenxia villages and were seen for several *li* before they disappeared.
1653:	Famine returned. Rice cost 8 cash a *dou*, and many starved to death.
1655, 21 November:	A violent hailstorm demolished houses and injured people.
1660, 9 December:	Seven days and nights of continuous thunderstorm.
1661, summer:	A white cloud over Red Flower Mountain looked from a distance like a flock of white sheep.
1662:	High tides caused flooding, and this year the evacuation of villages took place.
1664, February/March:	A comet was seen in the south-west and there was drought in spring and summer.
1665, 18 March:	Several circles of white vapour were seen round the sun and did not disperse for a long while.
1666, 20 November:	A comet was seen in the south-east. It was many yards long and looked like a rainbow.
1669, February/March:	High tides caused flooding as in 1662 and this year the villagers moved back.
28 July:	Three dragons, two white and one black rose up from the sea in the west and flew to the south of the city where they caused much damage to housing.
20 September:	A fearsome typhoon destroyed all the newly-built houses of the people who had just moved back to their villages.
1671, 21 March:	A great typhoon destroyed the city wall, the school-temple, the magistrate's yamen and a lot of private housing, and whole herds of cattle were blown into the sea.

1672: The white cloud reappeared on Red Flower Mountain just as in 1661.

1673, 5 July: A typhoon caused high tides which brought flooding, submerging housing and drowning the crops. The County Magistrate Li Kecheng offered prayers for relief. (See the literary extracts section.)

1677, May/June: The white vapour appeared on Qianlong Mountain as before.

17 September: There was a terrible typhoon in the night destroying the city wall, the yamen, and many private houses. A large number of people and livestock were crushed to death in the ruins.

1680: Large numbers of tigers caused many casualties, but the attacks ceased at the end of the year.

July/August: A comet was sighted in the west and remained visible for several months.

1686, 14 May: Torrential rain fell for days on end. The county city is on high ground but was still flooded and the drains could not cope with the water. The south and west gates were hastily thrown open to let out the water but it did not go down. The south-west corner of the city was under more than ten feet of water and not a house remained standing. The people went out in the rain and fled for their lives in all directions. There was unremitting devastation everywhere. The walls were breached in two places to give the water outlet, and when the flood was under control the people began to feel somewhat easier. Xixiang village west of the city had more than one hundred houses smashed down and washed into the sea. Yan village, Shuibei, Yongtou, and Huangsonggang in the north-west sector all had their mud walls and countless houses swept away. The people climbed on to their roofs and lashed bamboo and wood together to make rafts to escape on, but for the most part they were drowned, as were large numbers of animals. At Xinwei Village north of the city more than ten feet of water surrounded the mud walls and the people there also made good their escape on wooden rafts. The

	damage in the Zhu Village area of the northern sector was much the same. It is quite unnecessary to mention the devastation caused to fields and crops.
2 October:	Great pellets of hail fell. The autumn was dry and there was no rice harvest.

(All the above entries are taken from the old gazetteer.)

1708:	A great famine.
1757, 4 March:	At night there was a frost over one foot thick[44] and rice was expensive this year.
1760, 17 September:	A typhoon.
1761, 8 September:	A typhoon.
1768, 21-27 June:	Torrential rain non-stop.
1770, June/July:	Heavy rain.
2 September:	An earthquake.
1772:	Packs of wolves and tigers injured many people.
1777-78:	Two years of great drought. Rice was expensive and many people starved to death.
1786:	Locusts ate the rice crops. The autumn and winter were dry and there was famine.
1787:	Yet another drought. Rice cost one foreign dollar[45] a *dou* and many people died of starvation.
1788, March/April:	Hailstorms.
1791:	There was a succession of typhoons.
1797, July/August:	Four typhoons came in succession and many trees and houses were blown down.
1801, 18 March:	At night a star was seen to go into the moon and out again.
1802, 4 April:	Around 10 a.m. a white bow across the face of the sun.
1804, February/March/April:	Incessant rain, and salt became expensive. It cost twelve foreign dollars per catty.
1805, March:	A cloud of black vapour followed by one of red arose from the sea to the south-west of the city and disappeared off to the north-east. Violent winds suddenly tossed wayfarers over ten feet into the air, rendering them senseless, and their faces glowed as if on fire.
23 September:	Heavy rains caused flooding.

1807, 15 March:	A white halo round the sun.
18/19 March:	Hailstorms in the Kowloon/Haoyong area. Much livestock killed by it.
1811, 2 October:	At night a comet was seen in the north-west. It did not disappear until December.
1812:	Locusts ate the rice crop in the eastern sector of the county.
1814, September/October:	Hailstorm.
November/December:	Heavy rain.
1818, 8 October:	Heavy rain caused flooding, and bridges and embankments all were washed away in rivers of mud. Hill fields collapsed in landslides.

T.37

Bandits
寇盗

p.369

MING DYNASTY

1493:	Foreign barbarians constantly came to plunder, but Lieutenant Yuan Guang of the Dongguan Guard-post captured and put them to death at Cenzi'ao.
1516:	Foreign barbarians, the Franks,[46] came to plunder and occupied Tunmen Bay. The Naval Commander Wang Hong defeated them.
1533	Pirates led by Xu Zhegui and Wen Zongshan came to plunder. Lieutenant Gu Sheng of Dongguan Guard-post pursued them to Chunhuayang but was killed in battle. Afterwards the pirates were defeated by Naval Commander Jiang Liangcai (Jiang sent the County Magistrate Lin Qi[47] to sacrifice to Gu Sheng with the citation 'How brave was he! Why did not Heaven protect him?')
1551:	The pirate He Aba led barbarians to plunder. The Dongguan Commander Wan Li made a stand at Yandun on Nan Shan but was killed when the two sides met. Later Commander Li Maocai led an army against the bandits and destroyed them.
1566:	Huang Xiqiao and his bandits slaughtered and

pillaged through the countryside. Brigadier-General Yu Dayou put them down.

1567: The pirate Zeng Yiben came to plunder. Troops pursued him to Leizhougang where he was killed by Captain Li Maocai.[48]

1570: Japanese pirates plundered the villages of the county. Sergeant Wu Lun led militia against them but was killed in battle. Later Brigadier-General Guo exterminated the invaders.

1571: Japanese pirates attacked Dapeng City. When one of the inhabitants Kang Shoubo organized the defence of the city, it was besieged for more than forty days. The pirates were equipped with scaling ladders which they put up against the walls, but Kang encouraged his men to stout defence, any pirates who got to the top were cut down and their ladders smashed. So the siege was lifted and the authorities put up a tablet to honour Kang.

1580: The Laowan Shan bandits ravaged the area. The Coastal Defence Sub-prefect Zhou Xiyin dispatched troops who defeated them. Previously in 1569[49] this bandit gang had occupied Laowan Shan after being attacked and driven away by Sun Ao, the Commander for Defence against Japanese Pirates and by Naval Commander, Lin Mao. But then they had re-emerged to prey upon shipping. Sub-prefect Zhou's troops defeated them and destroyed their hideouts before returning to base.

1623: Red-haired barbarians in two great ships, their sails and masts shutting out the heavens, came brazenly in to moor below the temple at Fotangmen. The County Magistrate Tao Xuexiu in person led a force of armed militia to take up defensive positions at Xixi and elsewhere, whereupon the ships went away.

1630: The pirate Li Kuiqi came to plunder. Lieutenant-Colonel Chen Gong killed him but the pirates had more than a hundred ships and continued the raid. Chen and his coastal guards opposed them and in an engagement off Fotangmen he captured seven of their ships and executed the crews. The rest of the pirates were enraged and set course for Nantou. With so few men Chen could not stand against them, and he sought shelter within the city walls. The pirates then came ashore and prepared scaling ladders to attack the city. The defenders used red-hot weapons to kill the attackers and break their ladders. The siege was lifted, but the surrounding area was sacked and the Provincial Governor paid out 800 taels in compensation for the military and civilian casualties. The pirates' power waxed even stronger and they moved on to make their base at Dianbai and Lintaugong. The Governor ordered Chen to take command of a fleet of over a hundred assorted ships and get rid of them. Chen was jealous of sharing honour with colleagues, so he went ahead in the large vanguard junk. It was overcome right at the start of the battle and Chen was killed.

1633: The pirate Liu Xiang pillaged Fujian Province but was defeated in battle by General Zheng Zhilong. He fled before the wind and in March/April suddenly anchored at the Bocca Tigris where he put the fort's guards to the sword and thence harrassed the waterways of the province. General Zheng led a force to suppress him, defeated him in battle at Chigang and the pirates took to flight..

1634: Liu Xiang returned and on 15 June more than two hundred of his ships anchored off Nantou. Brigadier-General Deng led a force against them and captured a number of pirates. The rest hoisted sail and carried on their pillaging in Jiangmen in Xinhui County. On 27 July they appeared at Nantou yet again, but a typhoon happening to blow up, the government forces attacked with the wind behind them, defeating the pirates, who fled.

1635: Liu Xiang once more attacked Fujian but was beaten off by General Zheng Zhilong. Liu then took two local officials named Kang and Hong and held them hostage. In April/May he anchored off the county seat and demanded a ransom of charcoal, iron, rice and pork. The County Magistrate Wu

Wenming and the inhabitants secured their defences and would not pay up. Every night they lit torches and passed recognition tallies around. After more than a month of stalemate Liu set fire to the suburbs and the Magistrate swore an oath that his forces would make a sally to put out the flames. Captain Yu Zigao feasted the men with meat and wine after which they fought courageously causing the pirates to retreat a little. In June/July the local troops joined forces with General Zheng's men and met and defeated the pirates at Tianwei. The Prefect Xiong Wencau wrote a citation and ordered the County Magistrate to read it in sacrificing on the shore at Nantou to those soldiers killed in the battles.

1641, December: Bandits from Yinpingzui went on the rampage. With drums beating and banners flying they marched straight into Longyuetou Village. The inhabitants were terrified and reported the matter to the County Magistrate Zhou Xiyao. He drew up a secret plan and dispatched troops who captured more than thirty bandit chiefs, amongst them the one known as the 'Cotton Wool King'. Over three hundred heads were cut off and the matter was cleared up. Orders were issued to the local troops to pursue other bandits and very few in all those hills managed to escape. The Prefect memorialized that rewards for merit should be given.

PRESENT DYNASTY

1645, 2 December: The pirate Li Zhongguo and others named Xu, Zheng, Shi and Ma twice came looting through the area. The official troops and militia opposed them and drove them off plunderless.

1647: The bandit Chen Yao breached the Dapeng city wall, sacked the city and then departed. The bandit chief Li Wanrong then occupied the city while Luo Qinzan took the Meisha and Kuiyong area. They pillaged in all directions destroying more than half of all the houses in the county and killing or kidnapping tens of thousands of people. In 1654 Brigadier-General Wu went to pacify them but there was trouble with the navy, he was unsuccessful and recalled the troops. Later the two bandits fell out and Li killed Luo. In 1656 Brigadier-General Huang Yingjie with Liu Hong as a local guide led an army which surrounded Li on Dapeng Hill. After three months Li's supplies were exhausted and he surrendered and the district finally knew peace.

1664, September/October: A junior officer called Yuan Sidou rebelled and came into this area making his hideout at Liyuan in Guanfu District. From there he raided in all directions. Provincial Commander-in-Chief Yang ordered Major Wang to subdue him with a joint force of regulars and militia.

1672, October/November: The great traitor from Taiwan Li Qi and others led a fleet of pirate ships on a plundering expedition, and they came ashore at Haoyong and went through the villages looting and slaughtering. The County Magistrate Li Kecheng and Major Cai Chang assembled a force of village braves and regular troops which launched a joint offensive. The bandits realized that they were no match for this strong force but had no way of escaping. They took refuge in Liyuan and other places. Li Kecheng kept his troops on the move searching for them and the area became peaceful again when all had been captured or killed.

1676: Pirates came from Huiyang to plunder. They looted and killed in all the villages they passed through and finally occupied the county seat. It was not until the following year that possession of the city could be regained and the people live in peace.

1680, 25 June: At dawn pirates suddenly descended on Xixiang and Dayong. They looted until noon and then went away. On 26 June they anchored in Baishihai near Shajiang and they plundered the Xiacun area. Only the walled village of Jibailing offered resistance. After several days the crafty schemes of the pirates led to its fall and they put every one of its inhabitants to death. The only survivors were two or three who were away at the time.

1804: Guo Podai, Wu Shier, Zhang Yi and others scoured the coast looting and kidnapping the inhabitants. Those who were rich they held to ransom, the poor were forced to turn pirate. Their power grew daily and their pirate fleet of vessels large and small numbered over a thousand. Not only were they active on the water, they also plundered on dry land. Villages near the coast all maintained guards to defend themselves. Ping Shan, Guxu, Yongshujiao and Wanxia were all surrounded and attacked by the pirates, but were stoutly defended and the pirates retreated.

1808, 14 July: Scores of pirate ships pillaged the seas to the west of the county seat. Commander of the Left Lin Guoliang led nineteen ships against them but was killed in fierce fighting.

1809, November/December: Guo Podai and his pirates came in several hundred ships and anchored off Lantau, Chilijiao and other places in the county's jurisdiction. The County Magistrate Zheng Yushu personally led an armada of fishing boats against them. The Prefect Bai also mustered troops and several hundred ships. They blockaded the pirate anchorages, but unfavourable winds allowed the pirates to slip away.

1810: Prefect Bai persuaded the pirate Guo Podai and others to surrender, and the people of the sea-coast were thus freed from the alarms of the warning beacons and could return to their peaceful everyday occupations.

T.38

The Evacuation
遷復

p.374

FIRST STAGE

1661: As the coastal waters had not yet been pacified it

was proposed that the people of the coast should be moved away out of danger. Brigadier-General Zhang came and surveyed the whole coast.

1662, March/April: The Grand Commissioner set up a new boundary along the coast and two-thirds of the county's area was to be evacuated. In April/May Brigadier-General Cao, General Commandant Ma and regular troops were sent to realize the boundary and to expel the inhabitants from the area within 50 *li* of the coast. The people at first were ignorant of the new boundary and although proclamations had been posted up they only knew of the evacuation when the troops arrived. They had to leave most of their property and set off with their wives and children. Some died from sleeping out in the open, others sought refuge in Dongguan and Guishan Counties and yet others moved further on still and were scattered in many areas.

SECOND STAGE

1663, September: The Grand Commissioners Yi and Shi came again to inspect the Guangdong coastal territory with a view to extending the boundary and evacuating the entire county. Viceroy Lu pleaded that the complete evacuation should not be carried out as the population had already suffered great hardship in the first removal, and it was decided that only twenty-four villages in the east and west sectors should be evacuated. In March/April 1664, Military Commandant Jiang Hongrun and County Magistrate Zhang Pu drove the people of the twenty-four villages back behind the new boundary. Thereafter the Grand Commissioners came to inspect the coastal area once a quarter. At first the evacuees had high hopes of returning and could not bear to leave their wives and children. But as time went by they could not make a living and at this point men abandoned their wives, fathers their sons, brother parted from brother, and their wanderings and hardships were too many to be

	told. The officials at county and higher levels all worked to devise means to get employment for them but there were so many evacuees and so little of the county left that they were unable to help in fact.
RETURN	
1668, February/March:	Governor Wang petitioned for the restoration of the old territory. The Emperor sent a Commissioner to co-operate with Viceroy Zhou in supervising the extension and organizing its defences. The people's cheers filled the air and they came long distances to welcome the officials.
November/December:	Viceroy Zhou petitioned to open the area and set up defence installations.
1669, February/March:	The people were allowed to return to take up their occupations. Those who were at first unwilling heard that the people were happy and returned as if to a new life.
July/August:	The area reverted to full county status.

(All the above is to be found in the old gazetteer.)

T.39

Officials and their good works
官蹟略

p.377

Wang Hong, also known as Chengzhai, from Wuyuan in Huizhou, made Intendant of Circuit in 1521. Barbarian Franks on the pretext of bringing tribute occupied the port of Tunmen from where they made frequent sorties to plunder, slaughter and eat little children. The censors Qiu Daolong and He Ao successively memorialized and were given permission to expel them. Wang personally put to sea to direct the planned attack. He recruited and organized volunteer troops and led them into battle with righteous encouragement. Victorious he distributed all the spoils among his subordinates and took absolutely nothing for himself. He was promoted to President of the Board of War and Associate President of the Censorate. The people built a temple at Chongzhenli as thanks for his great efforts.[50] Now he is worshipped alongside Naval Commander Liu, his tablet having been entered in the Temple of Celebrated Officials in 1615.

p.378

Liu Wen, also called Renshan, a native of Ling County in Huguang Province. Took office as Intendant of Circuit in 1572. The county originally was part of Dongguan, but being over 100 *li* from the county's seat the Japanese and Western barbarian pirates were constantly able to gather to wreak havoc, and gangs of young hooligans publicly practised evil sacrifices. When he came to office he prohibited these, got rid of the idols and used the *Xiangyue* lecture system to reform them. Every 1st and 15th day of the lunar month he would observe the *Xiangyue* and have imperial edicts read out to the populace. At the request of Wu Zuo and others he reported to his superiors that the great distance between Dongguan City and this area made control difficult so that the people could do wrong with impunity, and the present county was established....

Wu Daxun; also called Runquan, from Maping in Guangxi, holder of the *suigongsheng* degree. Became County Magistrate in 1573. Generous and extremely kind, he threw himself wholeheartedly into setting up the new administration in the most suitable way.....bringing respect to the elderly and honour to men of culture, an excellent man to be magistrate. In 1615 his tablet was placed in the Temple of Celebrated Officials.

p.380

Ding Tangfa from Jia Shan in Zhejiang Province, holder of the *jinshi* degree, made County Magistrate in 1694. A man of kindness and compassion, he abolished poll-tax abuses, ran corvée service fairly and did away with whatever was not advantageous to the populace. There had never been a county school, and he organized the local gentry to build the Bao'an Academy. When he was promoted to another post the gentry and elders of the county had a stone erected commemorating his rule. It still stands within the south gate of the city. His tablet is in the temple.

Jin Qizhen, Plain-white Bannerman, a *jiansheng*, made County Magistrate in 1700. Upright, intelligent and benevolent, as soon as he got to post he looked to the sufferings of the people. At that time it was not long after the county's evacuation and the people were in distress. If anyone had failed to pay taxes, his whole clan was held responsible, but Jin was compassionate and laid down that the *jia* unit should be established with names of individuals clearly recorded. If someone had accumulated debts which he could not pay only the one man need be held guilty, so that the people could go about their occupations with a quiet mind. Also during his rule the waterways were badly silted up, and great floods brought terrible suffering to the people. He arranged for the dredging of the channels and all the water disasters were abated, effects which have lasted down to the present day. His tablet is in the temple.

p.382

Zhou Xiyao, also called Daosheng, from Jingde in Jiangnan, holder of the *juren* degree, appointed County Magistrate in 1640. He was greatly concerned about the sufferings of the people and with giving encouragement to the training of men of ability. He was skilful in handling the economy, methodical and capable in all his administration, and well acquainted with the facts of the hardships which affected the people. He dealt with the evils of the day by such measures as reviving the fishing and salt industries in order to give local people a livelihood again, stabilizing prices out of compassion for the itinerant traders, co-ordinating the granaries so as to abolish abuses, and forbidding squeeze so as to stop corruption — all examples of good administration. Seeing that very few men from Xin'an passed the civil service examinations, he used the large site of the old academy at Wengang outside the east gate facing Beidu and regardless of the difficulties built a new school there. Thereafter generations of good scholars were produced and everyone has benefited by it.

p.384

Li Kecheng, also called Jiyou, from Tieling in Liaodong, holder of a *juren* degree under the official entry quota,[51] appointed County Magistrate in 1670. A benevolent and upright man, he came to office at the beginning of the return to the coastal territory after evacuation. The suffering people had not yet all returned. He gave every encouragement to them to return by offering cattle and seed, supervision of farming and exhortation to study. The dilapidated walls and moats and government offices were repaired by donation without imposing a burden on the common people. He also put in hand the strengthening of the existing defences as a means of protecting the people, and he personally supervised the levying of taxes, doing away with abuses in the collection with the result that the people were happy to pay. When he received a report that a powerful bandit called Li Qi had come to pillage he immediately in person led a joint force of militia and official troops and brought about their total suppression....

p.385

Zhang Mingda, also called Zishang, from Shenyang in Fengtian Prefecture, a *jiansheng*, made County Magistrate in 1678. He encouraged the suffering people to move back and then cared for them. The school was in ruins and he repeatedly asked the authorities for money for restoration, but without success. Finally he appealed to the gentry for donations, and after a few years the work was done and the temple rebuilt. In 1681 a population census was decreed and he gave strict orders to all those concerned that there was to be no harrassment of the people. Contemporary opinion held him in high esteem.

Jin Wenmo, also called Qiyuan, from Kaizhou in Zhili, a *jinshi*, made County Magistrate in 1687. From the moment he took office he set about reforming and correcting everything which was not as it should be, and the people were made at ease by this. He was liberal, kind, magnanimous and hard-working and he busied himself in administration from morning to night. He undertook much restoration and building of the city walls, forts and quarters, and when the drumtower of the county seat was destroyed in a typhoon and he had unsuccessfully asked the authorities for money, he solicited donations and restored it to its former state. In law cases he made it his job to get to the truth and he encouraged the people to be frugal and live a simple life. The people claimed that even the good officials of old were not superior to him.

T.40

Historic sites
古蹟

p.460

The Jingyan Travelling Palace: In 1277 the Song Jingyan Emperor came to Meiwei Hill[52] and established his travelling palace there.

The Song Travelling Court at Guanfu: It is recorded that in May/June 1277 the Emperor came by sea and stayed here. The foundations and some stone pillars of the palace still remain, but the local people have now used them as the foundation of the Beidi Temple.

The Song King's Terrace: To the east of Guanfu there is a flat rock a score or more feet square. It was here in the past that the emperor Dibing stayed. Beside the terrace is a great rock on which used to be the three words 'Song King's Terrace'.[53]

p.463

Waiting Wife Rock (Amah Rock): Near the shore at Liyuan. On her back is a smaller stone like a child being carried there.

Beidu Hill, coastal beauty spot: In the Former Song dynasty[54] the Buddhist Monk Beidu settled here and hence its name. At the foot of the hill are two stone columns 40 paces apart and 17 metres high, but they are now broken off half-way down. The prefectural gazetteer says that long ago a whale swam into these waters and broke them by butting into them. Midway up the hill is the Beidu Monastery, in front of which is the Running Tiger Spring with Deer Lake, Peach Blossom Stream, Dripping Water Crag, Heaven's Blessing Crag and Golden Oriole Rock on its left. Behind it is Stone Buddha Crag on which is a stone statue of Beidu. Behind that is a cave of immeasurable depth and two bell-flower trees. Surrounding the top of the crag is a large grove of ancient trees, their dark foliage a green mosaic of splendour. There also is Orchid Bloom Path with fragrance which lasts throughout the year. At the top of the hill are carved the four characters 'Greatest of High Mountains' and there is an old tradition that they were written by Han Yu.[55]

T.41

Notable people (1)
人物

p.482

Deng Konglin, also known as Guorui, a filial and hard-working man. In the Ming Wanli reign period[56] his father Gongzuo was abducted by the pirate Lin Feng. Konglin immediately went to the pirate ship and offered himself in his father's place, whereupon his father was released. Konglin sailed with the pirates, but when they came to port in Haifeng he watched for a moment when his captors relaxed their vigilance, got off to the shore by floating on a piece of wood, and so escaped back home. His fellow-villagers all praised him and remarked how Heaven protects the filial son. They reported the matter to the county authorities and the County Magistrate Qiu Liqian[57] presented him with an honours board inscribed 'His filial conduct is acclaimed at Court' and also with gifts of rice and cloth. When he died, further citations were granted to his descendants to grace their door.

p.491

Liu Junpei, a commoner of this county, conducted himself in a most righteous manner. In 1633 it befell that brigands were about to slaughter his brother's grandson Kemei. Junpei said: 'My late nephew has only this one son to carry on his line. I have a son, so it would be better to kill me.' The brigands slew him but spared both his son and his brother's grandson. It was decreed that he should be worshipped in the Hall of Loyalty and Righteousness.

p.493

Huang Chenglian from Dapeng held the post of Sergeant of the Dapeng Left Patrol. In 1789 while on a naval exercise to Annam he met up with pirates and was killed in battle. In was decreed that in his honour his younger brother should be granted the title *Feng'enqiwei* 鳳恩騎尉.

T.42

Notable people (2)
人物

p.498

Miss Wu, daughter of Wu Yuanming of the county's second regiment of infantry. In 1635 there was an attack by the pirate Liu Xiang. Miss Wu and her mother fled for safety to the foot of Nan Shan where they were captured by a pirate who tried to rape the girl, but she was incensed, picked up a stone and attacked him, wounding his nose. In fury he slew her out of hand. Everyone praised her for her chaste virtue.

p.499

Miss Chen, betrothed wife of Zeng Nengchao. At the age of twenty she received news of his death and preserved her chastity for life. In 1730 she was officially honoured for this.

p.501

Deng Zhaoguang's widow, née He, remained chaste for life. In 1706 she was officially honoured for it.

p.506

Miss Liao, betrothed wife of Wu An. Wu An died before the wedding had taken place, and when she heard the news she hanged herself. Her elder brother

Liao Wanqiao had her body encoffined and sent to be buried alongside Wu.

p.511

Juren Zhang Dunxin's widow, née Deng. After six years of marriage her husband died when she was twenty-seven years of age. She maintained chaste widowhood, served her parents-in-law with full filial piety and had her son educated at the county academy where he did very well. She is now fifty-eight years old.

T.43

Notable people (3)
人物

p.535

Huang Renjing of the Beitou area of Nantou lived to the age of ninety-nine.

Liao Henggu of Shangshui lived to the age of one hundred. In 1736 the Provincial Governor Yang Yongbin presented him with an honorific board bearing the words 'A hundred years of service'.

p.536

Shangshui jiansheng Liao Dingbang's wife, née Li. Lived to one hundred and one years old. In 1787 she was officially honoured with a memorial arch on which was the inscription 'Virtuous and Excelling'.

Deng Fu, also known as Deng Fuxie, from Jishui County in Jiangxi Province. Became a *jinshi* during the Song Changning period[58] and was honoured with the title *Chengwulang*. He was appointed Magistrate of Yangchun County in the South District. Enamoured of the beauty of the local scenery he chose to settle down in this county at Jintian near the foot of Guijiao Hill. He built the Liying School there and encouraged people to study: Huo Wei of Nanhai wrote an account of it. Deng's great-grandson Ziming married a daughter of the Song Gaozong Emperor[59] and their descendants have lived on in Jintian, Longyuetou, Pingshan, Zhucun, Xiacun and other places where they have now developed into an influential clan.[60]

p.537

Tan Gongdao from Guishan County settled on Jiulong Hill in this county, and lived a hermit's life. His dates are not recorded. Whenever this venerable man went out onto the hillside a tiger would follow along behind him and sometimes it would accompany him carrying loads of vegetables on its back. After his death, when people prayed to him for rain or for sun they invariably got it. (Copied in from the Guishan Gazetteer.)

T.44

Memorial: reopen the closed area and let the people return.

展界復鄉疏

From Governor Wang Lairen

p.551

It is a matter of urgency that the closed area of Guangdong should be opened up. The province is hemmed in by mountains and sea and its territory is at best small, but now after the two evacuations from the coastal region there are tens of thousands of evacuees, and this represents an annual loss of revenue from land and poll-taxes of more than 300,000 taels. Furthermore, with the population moved out, large numbers of troops have to be stationed at many points to guard the area. The fortresses and stockades which were built to hold the territory require constant supplies of manpower and materials to keep them in good order. It costs more than can be afforded and none of this is paid for from the public purse, it is all dependent upon the efforts of the people. Thus, those who have not been evacuated are daily forced to hard labour, while those who have been evacuated have nowhere to settle and many deaths are reported. Is there no way to make the people's lives easy? I beg that the ban on residence in the evacuated territory be lifted; that the people be encouraged to return to take up their farming and salt production; that the booms be removed from the rivers and harbours to allow the people to fish where they choose; and that the troops be withdrawn from inland areas and redeployed in the administrative cities along the coast as a defence against attack from the sea. These measures must be in the national interest, Your Majesty's lands will not lie needlessly abandoned, and the benefit to the people will be enormous .... I have been Governor of Guangdong for more than two years and in that time have not heard a single instance of major attack by pirate forces — such banditry as there has been has been perpetrated inland by gangs of evacuees. If we were now to reopen the area these brigands would sell their weapons and buy cattle ....

T.45

Petition to relieve the hardships of the pearl-fishers
上宣慰司採珠不便狀

Zhang Weiyin (Yuan dynasty)

p.553

I have seen with my own eyes how the people engaged in pearl-fishing are made to suffer by the officials in charge of them ...... Liu Chang enlisted a force of 3,000 pearl-fishers at Haimenzhen which he called the Meichuandou. Every year many were drowned, and the practice was stopped for this reason. The story is that during the Five Dynasties period Liu Chang, the ruler of the non-legitimate Nan Han, occupied Guangzhou, but the first emperor of the Song dynasty sent General Pan Mei (in February/March 971) to reduce Guangzhou, and he received Liu Chang's surrender. By June/July 972 the Meichuandou had been abolished. It was not that the emperor was unaware of the value of the pearls, but he realized that he must put an end to this most harmful practice with all possible speed. What the Five Dynasties people called a *Dou* is what we now call an Army Wing. If the good divers had all gone pearl-fishing what need would there have been for conscripting a force of 3,000 men? The only way in which they could bring the people to the deadly work in fact was by military force. The pearls are produced in oysters which are found at a depth of several hundred feet, and where the pearls are most numerous there are water monsters and fearsome fish protecting them. For a fast descent to get the pearls the men are let down on a rope weighted with a stone. The divers sometimes find oysters and sometimes not, but in either case when their air is used up they jerk the rope and the men in the boat haul them up quickly — a little too late and the divers bleed from all their apertures and die. And sometimes inevitably they are devoured by fierce fish and water monsters. What is worse is that out of every hundred or so oysters opened there are no more than one or two which contain pearls! ...... The reason why Liu Chang organized his *Dou* of 3,000 men was to control the divers lest they should ruin things by running away and scattering afar. The so-called 'conscripting as soldiers' was in fact 'driving to the slaughter'. In view of this he had no choice but to be lavish with clothing, food and accommodation not only for the men but for their wives and children also, and whatever annual profit was made on the pearls was not enough to meet the costs of supporting these troops.

T.46

Bring an end to violence so as to bring peace to the people

戢囂爭以安民

Zhou Xiyao

p.560

It can be seen that this county lies between two important areas, and nearly all the best land has been taken by their powerful men. In this way the blessings all go to the neighbours and the people of Xin'an have only the hardships.

There are two major evils. The first is 'fighting for markets'. On market days the people who go there on behalf of the profiteers commit murder and arson. Cases have been taken to court again and again through the years but always there have been recurrences soon after. Gangs of armed men pillage and murder, and it is always the people of Xin'an who suffer.

The second is 'fighting for fields'. Every plot of land has its designated owner, so who could take it away? The answer is these powerful men who either force people to give them the land under duress or cook up false documents and make use of official insignia to take illegal occupation of the land, banging gongs and letting off firearms to intimidate, extorting rental, killing and maiming the tenant farmers. Again it is Xin'an people who suffer.

Alas for our people! What harm have they done that they should deserve such evil? They are the ones who have settled the territory, but those who fight and those who fight with them are from the neighbouring counties, supported and encouraged by their gentry, and the people are powerless to stop them. I have responsibility for this county, and I feel for the people's suffering. If I tolerated these evils there would be no hope for the people and I should be to blame. Therefore I beg that there should be strict prohibition on such activities and that the yamens concerned should exact heavy punishment, seeking out and arresting a few of the ringleaders, and bringing them to justice. Then the bullies will cease their activities, this will put an end to the fighting, and the people of Xin'an may all settle down in peace.

T.47

Register the Tanka so as to stop the supply of pirates

編蛋甲以塞盜源

Zhou Xiyao

p.564

It has been found that a lot of piratical activity is carried on by the Tanka, so if we are to rid ourselves of these pirates we must first enquire carefully into the position of the Tanka. What is the well-spring of their piracy? It is that they can go around freely wherever they want on the sea. In the morning they are in the east, by night they are in the west, and they anchor wherever they like. Sometimes eight or nine, sometimes more than ten boats operate together as a fleet to fish, the fleet being known as a 'fellowship of the net' (*gupeng* 罟朋). Each *gupeng* is followed by a mother-ship which salts down the catch and carries provisions for the fishing boats. All the latter take their catch to the mother-ship and for both sides this is an excellent arrangement. But a mother-ship properly going about its business may suddenly spot an isolated merchantman or fishing boat and then it will seize the chance to organize its fleet of boats to attack and they take goods instead of fish. Those in authority have told them again and again to desist, but the best way to put an end to this piracy is through *baojia* organization. It is hereby proposed that ten boats should form a *jia* under a *jia*-headman, and three *jia* should form a *bao* under a *bao*-headman, and all boats, large, small and mother-ships alike, no matter how remote the area, alone or in company, in *gupeng* or not, shall form *jia* and *bao* and register themselves. They will watch over each other and be held mutually responsible for wrongdoing. When the *baojia* system is operated strictly it will be hard for law-breaking boats to slip off and it follows that the pirate scourge will soon be swept away, and the source of piracy stopped up.

T.48

Proposal to reduce grain stocks
詳減積穀

Zhou Xiyao

p.568

Clearly it is of prime importance to keep stores of grain and to give orders for contributions to be made and reserves accumulated. This is our duty as officials and we should not shirk it. But conditions in different counties vary, the people may be affluent or poverty-stricken: what applies in general may not apply to one particular case. This county, far from producing a surplus of grain, has difficulty in buying what it needs. I have orders to store 1,000 *dan* a year and to make reports on stocks every quarter. From last winter to this summer I have already collected 1,750 *dan* plus money rendered in lieu of grain but it is still not enough to pay wages and I have several times had to borrow to make up the full amount. This quarter's report is quite clear and needs no amplification. The trouble is that the county is not a productive one, the people are poor, the cultivated area small and tax revenue sparse. As can be seen from previous records, 25 taels worth have to be deducted from the spring and summer amounts as pay for the army; and in addition in autumn and winter a fifth of the stocks, namely 7 taels 5 cash have to be taken for the ministry, and a total of more than 40 taels for aid to the counties of Nanhai and Panyu, for payments to granary officials, for oil, candles and stationery for the courts, for prison rations, etc. What remains to be stored even after additional receipts is only 150 *dan*, and now I am ordered to store 1,000 *dan* a year! The cost of 150 *dan* is only 37 taels 5 cash, but this 1,000 *dan* would cost 250 taels! This is a huge increase over the old figure! ...... The county lies on the coast, it is small and the people are poor. I beg that this will be borne in mind and that it will generously be permitted for the amount of grain to come down to 100 *dan* per quarter.

T.49

Strictly enforce the baojia system to keep crime in check
嚴保甲以稽奸

p.573 *Li Kecheng*

It is known that the *baojia* system has long been established here but it has not been enforced and corrupt practices abound. It is better to be severe at first than to have to punish later, so now groups of ten families shall be registered as *jia* and ten *jia* shall constitute a *bao*. *Bao*-headmen shall be men commonly acknowledged to be of high virtue. Boards shall be displayed for each ten families showing the number of members, and the *bao*-headman shall make frequent visits of inspection. Should there be bandits or gamblers they must immediately make a report and have them arrested; and if there is any emergency in their area they should contact relief teams and give every support. On the 1st and 15th of every month the *bao*-headmen are to go to the county town and make a sworn statement of occurrences. ....

T.50

Commemorative stone for the building of the Fenggang Academy
新建鳳岡書院碑文

Xu Sun of Wu Jin, Assistant Prefectural Magistrate

p.607

...... The county lies right on the coast and its inhabitants are farmers and fishermen, but they are not unmindful of study. Thus the old gazetteer records the existence of a Bao'an Academy (now long since derelict) and in the south-west corner of the city there was the Wengang Academy, of which only the foundations survive, the rest having fallen down with age. In 1802 the former County Magistrate Wang[61] took advantage of the abandonment of the Dongguan Salt Offices in the city, subscribed a major sum, encouraged all the local gentry to come in with smaller amounts, and so was able to purchase the site for the Fenggang Academy. Work was begun in February/March 1803 and completed in March/April 1806. I happened to come to office at that time,[62] and wanting to promote culture and men of worth I looked for ways to provide scholarship money. I found that local people such as Liu Zhuanghua had in the past given endowments of land specifically for academic purposes, but fluctuations in the rental income had made disbursements unreliable. Now I have cleared up the accounts and after payment of essential charges all other moneys are to go to the academy for its use. Accordingly I have drawn up the regulations controlling income and expenditure and they are to be permanently displayed here.

APPENDIX

TABLE OF CONTENTS OF THE 1688 EDITION OF THE GAZETTEER

Jin Wenmo, Deng Wenwei *et al.* (comp.) 靳文謨，鄧文蔚, *Chongxiu Xin'an xianzhi* 重修新安縣志 [Revised Xin'an County Gazetteer], 1688.

CONTENTS	*NOTES*
	The title of this work is given variously as *Xin'an xianzhi* (Xin'an County Gazetteer) and as the longer title given above.
Prefatory Material	
Preface by Jin Wenmo 序	Dated '3rd winter month 1688'. Jin was County Magistrate at the time.
Notes on revision of the gazetteer 修志凡例	Dated '2nd winter month 1688'.
Contents of the gazetteer 目錄	
Chapter One — Maps 輿圖志	One of the county, one of Xin'an City. Distances to the county boundaries are given.
Chapter Two — Of the Heavens 天文志	
Geographical position 星野	
Climate 氣候	
Winds 風異	
Weather-lore 占候	Month by month.
Chapter Three — Of the Earth 地理志	
History of the county 沿革	From earliest times.

Walled cities 城池: Xin'an Dapeng	Locations, street names, barracks, circumference of walls, etc.
Territory 封域	Boundaries with other counties.
Villages 都里	Arranged under *dou* 都 .
Markets 墟市	
Ferries 津	
Bridges 梁	
Mountains 山	Includes caves, peaks, ridges, passes, cliffs and strange stone formations.
Waters 海	Includes seas, islands and streams.
Wells and springs 井泉	
Historic sites 古蹟	
Famous landmarks 八景	
Graves 丘墓	
Customs 風俗	
Products 方產	
Rices	
Wheats	
Pulses	
Vegetables	
Fruits	
Teas	
Medicines	
Bamboos	
Trees	
Flowers	
Grasses	
Animals	
Birds	
Fish	
Shellfish	
Insects	
Miscellaneous	Includes salt, indigo, sesame, etc.

Chapter Four — Officials 職官志

Civil establishment 文官制
Military establishment 武官制
List of civil officials 文官表
List of military officials 武官表

Chapter Five — Official Buildings 宮室志	
Civil offices 文署	
Military offices 武署	
Miscellaneous offices 雜署	Includes the Guanfu District offices, granaries, and salt centres.
Schools 學校	
annexe: endowments of land for educational purposes	
Charity schools	
Local schools	
Shrines 壇壝	
Temples 廟祠	
Post stations 郵舖	
Memorial arches 坊牌	All dilapidated.
Formal gardens 臺榭	
Chapter Six — Taxation 田賦志	
Population 戶口	
Land areas 土田	
Land-tax 賦	
Corvée 役	
Salt-tax 鹽課	
Fish-tax 魚課	
Miscellaneous taxes 雜餉	
Military farmland 屯田	
Chapter Seven — Ceremonial 典禮志	Details of the ceremonies to be held in the various temples.
Chapter Eight — Military and Punitive 兵刑志	
The military system 軍制	
Armaments 戎器	
Stockades 墪堡	The military posts and deployment of soldiery at them; the ships in use for sea defence. Arranged under Donglu 東路 and Xilu 西路 (Eastern Marches and Western Marches) which appear to have been under the control of Dapeng and Xin'an respectively.

Nantou Commandery 南頭寨
Watch posts 汎地
The fleet 寨船
Regular troops 寨兵
Irregular troops 兵壯
Punishment system 刑制 — The penalties and instruments of punishment (such as whips) available for use.

Chapter Nine — Preferment 選擧志
Recommended to the throne 薦辟
Jinshi 甲科
Juren 鄉科
Suigongsheng 歳貢
Enjian 恩監
Titles of honour 封爵

Chapter Ten — People 人物志
Famous officials 名宦
Local worthies 鄉賢
Righteous characters 行誼
Men of loyalty and courage 忠勇
Virtuous women 列女傳
Recluses 隱逸
Knight errants 游俠
Sojourners 僑寓

Chapter Eleven — Defence 防省志
Charities administration 卹政
Natural disasters 災異
Bandits 寇盗
The evacuation 遷復

Chapter Twelve — Literary Excerpts 藝文志
Memorials and proposals 條議
Commemorative writings 紀述
Belles-lettres 題咏

Chapter Thirteen — Miscellaneous 雜志
Temples and monasteries 寺廟
Mystics 僊釋

GLOSSARY OF HONG KONG PLACE NAMES

This list gives the Cantonese readings of Hong Kong place names mentioned in the text. Spellings are according to the Hong Kong Government's *A gazetteer of place names in Hong Kong, Kowloon and the New Territories.*

Beiwei 北圍 = Pak Wai
Changzhou 長洲 = Cheung Chau
Dabu 大埔 = Tai Po
Daguling 打鼓嶺 = Ta Kwu Ling
Damao Shan 大帽山 = Tai Mo Shan
Dayu Shan 大嶼山 = Tai Yue Shan (Lantau)
Fenling 粉嶺 = Fanling
Fotangmen 佛堂門 = Fat Tong Mun
Heshangxiang 河上鄉 = Ho Sheung Heung
Jishuimen 急水門 = Kap Shui Mun
Jintian 錦田 = Kam Tin
Jiulong 九龍 = Kowloon
Liyumen 鯉魚門 = Lei Yue Mun
Lincun 林村 = Lam Tsuen
Longyuetou 龍躍頭 = Lung Yeuk Tau
Matouwei 馬頭圍 = Ma Tau Wai
Meiwo 梅窩 = Mui Wo
Nanwei 南圍 = Nam Wai
Pingshan 屏山 = Ping Shan
Putai 蒲台 = Po Toi
Shatian 沙田 = Sha Tin
Shatoujiao 沙頭角 = Sha Tau Kok
Shangshui 上水 = Sheung Shui
Shaojiwan 筲箕灣 = Shau Kei Wan
Shenzhen 深圳 = Sham Chun
Shihuxu 石湖墟 = Shek Wu Hui
Taikeng 泰坑 = Tai Hang
Taiping Shan 太平山 = Tai Ping Shan
Tunmen 屯門 = Tuen Mun
Wangjing 輞井 = Mong Tseng
Xiacun 厦村 = Ha Tsuen
Xintian 新田 = San Tin
Yuanlang 元朗 = Yuen Long

NOTES

INTRODUCTION

1 Endacott, *A History of Hong Kong*, pp.17-22.
2 *Guangdong tongzhi*, vol. 1, pp.1454-55.
3 Ingrams, *Hong Kong*, p.152.
4 See *T.36*, AD 1629.
5 Chapter Seven.
6 Nivison, *The Life and Thought of Chang Hsüeh-ch'eng*, pp.48-49. See also Hummel, *Eminent Chinese of the Ch'ing Period*, pp.38-41.
7 See He, 'Lun fangzhi zai shijizhongde diwei ji gongyong'.
8 i.e. *T.36*, *T.37* and *T.38*.
9 Barnett, *Hong Kong before the Chinese*, pp.66-67.
10 See Ng, 'The San On Map of Mgr. Volonteri', and Hayes, 'The San On Map of Mgr. Volontieri [sic.]'.
11 Xue and Ouyang, A *Sino-Western Calendar for Two Thousand Years, AD* 1-2000.

1. HISTORY

1 See *Hong Kong 1981*, pp.230-31.
2 *The Journal of the Hong Kong Archaeological Society*, published annually through the Hong Kong City Museum and Art Gallery, carries up-to-date reports on work in progress. For some pioneering work see Finn, *Archaeological Finds on Lamma Island near Hong Kong*, and Meacham, *Archaeology in Hong Kong.*
3 *Xin'an xianzhi*, p.67.
4 See Wiens, *Han Chinese Expansion in South China*, p.39.
5 Ibid., p.114.
6 See *Beijing Review*, no.6, p.18.
7 See *T.10*. Also Wiens, op.cit., pp.132-33 and his maps 6 and 19.
8 *Xin'an xianzhi*, p.67.
9 Wiens, op.cit., pp.133-34.
10 See *T.10*.
11 Translated in Balfour, 'Hong Kong before the British', p.148.

12 Schafer, *The Vermilion Bird*, p.34.
13 *Guangdong wenwu*, vol. 2, *juan* 6, p.17.
14 Ibid., vol. 3, *juan* 8, p.7.
15 Lo, *Hong Kong and its External Communications before 1842*, p.21.
16 *Xin Tang shu*, *juan* 43, p.1153.
17 Han Yu, *Han Changli ji*, *juan* 6, no.6.
18 See *T.40*.
19 Quoted from *Minshuiyan tanlu*, see Lo, *Yibasiernian yiqian zhi Xianggang jiqi duiwai jiaotong*, p.57.
20 See *T.45* and also Lo, *Hong Kong and its External Communications before 1842*, ch.3 for more details.
21 Wiens, op.cit., pp.179-80.
22 Siak, 'Traditional Farming Techniques and their Survival in Hong Kong', p.192.
23 Barnett, 'Hong Kong before the Chinese', p.50.
24 Barnett, 'Introduction' to *Hong Kong Gazetteer*, and also 'Do Words from Extinct Pre-Chinese Languages Survive in Hong Kong Place-names?'.
25 See Xiang, *Man Shu jiaozhu*, pp.216-17.
26 Lim, 'Nan-Song shi Dayu Shan wei Yaoqu zhi shizhen'.
27 Wiens, op.cit., p.39. And see *T.5* for an instance of official Chinese attitudes to the Dan.
28 See Ho, 'A Study of the Boat People (with 5 maps)'.
29 See Ward, 'A Hong Kong Fishing Village', p.195.
30 Barnett, 'Hong Kong before the Chinese', pp.48-49.
31 Balfour, op.cit., p.160.
32 There is a discrepancy with regard to this date between *Xin'an xianzhi* (see *T.43(c)*) and the *Bao'an Jintian Dengshi zupu*. It could well be that the later date given in the gazetteer is nearer the truth.
33 See Baker, 'The Five Great Clans of the New Territories', p.28.
34 See Sung, 'Legends and Stories of the New Territories: Kam T'in' for more details on the Jintian Deng lineage.
35 Hayes, *The Hong Kong Region 1850-1911*, pp.47ff.
36 Baker, op.cit., p.26. See also Baker, *A Chinese Lineage Village* and Watson, *Emigration and the Chinese Lineage.*
37 Wong, 'Zhongyuan minzu zhi nanqian yu Guangdong wenhua zhi fazhan', p.8.
38 *Guangdong tongzhi*, *juan* 185.
39 Lim, op.cit., pp.186-87. Note that Balfour wrongly places these events later in history, see his 'Hong Kong before the British', pp.169-70.
40 See *T.40* and for a full account see Lo, *Hong Kong and its External Com-*

munications before 1842, pp.61-79. The same article with an additional map appears as Lo, 'The Sung Wang T'ai and the Location of the Travelling Courts by the Sea-shore in the Last Days of the Sung'.

41 Lo discusses the evidence for this (with some scepticism) in his *Yibasiernian yiqian zhi Xianggang jiqi duiwai jiaotong*, note 19, pp.85-87. It may be significant that there are also three Houwang temples on Lantau Island.

42 Ibid., pp.105-107.

43 *Guangdong wenwu, juan* 8, p.7.

44 Ibid. See also *Xin'an xianzhi*, ch.19, 'Local Worthies'.

45 A stone pillar on which the Portuguese coat of arms was carved, used to mark newly discovered territories.

46 Braga, *China Landfall, 1513*, p.24 and p.54.

47 Ibid., p.53 and *T.39*.

48 Balfour, op.cit., p.174.

49 Ibid., p.171 and Braga, op.cit., p.73.

50 See *T.34*.

51 See *T.37*.

52 See Lo, *Hong Kong and its External Communications before 1842*, pp.93ff and Hsieh, 'Removal of Coastal Population in Early Tsing Period'.

53 See *T.38* for details.

54 Hsieh, op.cit., p.591.

55 Qu, *Guangdong xinyu, juan* 2, pp.57-58.

56 See *T.10*, *T.38* and *T.44*.

57 See *T.21*.

58 See Sung, op.cit., vol. 14 (1974) p.185 and Baker, 'The Five Great Clans of the New Territories', p.38 and notes.

59 See *T.22*.

60 See Lo, *Hong Kong and its External Communications before 1842*, p.84.

61 See *T.25*.

62 The Hakka/Cantonese composition is discussed in Hayes, op.cit., pp.28-31.

63 See *T.2*.

64 See Lo, *Yibasiernian yiqian zhi Xianggang jiqi duiwai jiaotong*, pp.151-70.

65 The standard work is Endacott, *A History of Hong Kong*, but there are many more.

2. GEOGRAPHY

1 District Commissioner, New Territories, *Annual Departmental Report, 1970-71*, p.5.

2 Grant, *The Soils and Agriculture of Hong Kong*, pp.3-4.

3 See *T.12*, *T.19* and *T.36*.

4 See *T.11*, but in fact a few settlements on Hong Kong and Lantau Islands do appear in *Chongxiu Xin'an xianzhi* at *juan* 3.
5 Identified as an old term for the present Causeway Bay. See Lo, *Hong Kong and its External Communications before 1842*, pp.82-83.
6 For example see Baker, *A Chinese Lineage Village*, pp.45-46.
7 See *T.15* and *T.16* for more details.
8 *Chongxiu Xin'an xianzhi*, *juan* 3, p.15a-b. See Map 1.
9 See Hsiao, *Rural China: Imperial Control in the Nineteenth Century*, p.12 and Appendix I, especially p.522.
10 Indeed at the end of chapter 2 there is a comment that the old system had become difficult to understand as a result of administrative changes and place name alterations. See *T.14*.
11 See *T.14* The term actually used here is 本籍 'indigenously registered' rather than 本地人 'indigeni', but both are used to distinguish speakers of Cantonese from those who speak Hakka or other languages.
12 *Xin'an xianzhi*, ch.2.
13 See *T.30*.
14 See also *T.18*.
15 See Hayes, *The Hong Kong Region 1850-1911*, p.164.
16 *Xin'an xianzhi*, p.95.
17 See Lo, *Yibasiernian yiqian zhi Xianggang jiqi duiwai jiaotong*, p.146. note 17; also Baker, op.cit., p.30, and *T.37*.
18 See *T.13*.
19 See Baker, op.cit., photo, p.66 and pp.154-61, also Potter, *Capitalism and the Chinese Peasant, pp.20-21, and* Baker, *More Ancestral Images*, pp.137-40.
20 See *T.13*, also Baker, *Ancestral Images*, pp.25-28, and *Ancestral Images Again*, pp.29-31
21 See *T.13*.
22 See Baker, *More Ancestral Images*, pp.6-8.
23 See *T.25*.
24 Qu, *Guangdong xinyu*, pp.485-86.
25 More details on the Tanka can be found in Burkhardt, *Chinese Creeds and Customs*.
26 Kani, *A General Survey of the Boat People in Hong Kong*, pp.67-68. For confirmation of this view in the linguistic field see McCoy, 'The Dialects of Hong Kong Boat People: Kau Sai'.
27 Hayes, op.cit., pp.31-32.
28 Balfour, 'Hong Kong before the British', p.146; Burkhardt, *Chinese Creeds and Customs*, vol.2, p.85; and De Groot, *The Religious System of China*, vol. 5, pp.532-34.

29 See *T.5* and *T.47*.
30 See Lo, 'Communal Strife in Mid-nineteenth Century Kwangtung'.
31 Hayes, op.cit., p.40, and Char and Kwock, *The Hakka Chinese — their Origin and Folk Songs*, p.4.
32 Char and Kwock, op.cit., p.8.
33 See the Japanese translation of Lo, *Kejia yanjiu taolun*, map, p.98.
34 Hashimoto, *The Hakka Dialect: A Linguistic Study of its Phonology, Syntax and Lexicon*, p.1.
35 Hayes, op.cit., p.30.
36 *T.4*.
37 *T.5* and *T.7*.
38 *T.6*.
39 *T.49*.
40 T.3.
41 *T.13*.
42 *T.48*.
43 *T.42* and *T.43*.
44 *T.44* and *T.46*.

3. ECONOMY

1 Peplow and Barker, *Hongkong, Around and About*, p.17.
2 Grant, *The Soils and Agriculture of Hong Kong*, p.121.
3 *Xin'an xianzhi*, p.121.
4 Ibid., p.122.
5 Ho, *Studies on the Population of China, 1368-1953*, pp.186-87. See also Chang, *Food in Chinese Culture: Anthropological and Historical Perspectives, passim.*
6 See *T.3*.
7 *Xin'an xianzhi*, p.123.
8 Ibid., p.122.
9 Ibid., p.128.
10 Ibid., p.156.
11 See *T.36*.
12 See *T.9*.
13 Hsiao, *Rural China: Imperial Control in the Nineteenth Century*, pp.145-46. See also pp.144-83 and pp.549-52.
14 See *T.32*.
15 See *T.48*.
16 See *T.8*.
17 *Dan* 石 'picul' was a measure of grain equivalent to approximately 110 pounds weight.

18 Krone, 'A Notice of the San On District', p.121.
19 Ch'ü, *Local Government in China under the Ch'ing*, pp.159-60.
20 *Xin'an xianzhi*, pp.276-77.
21 Huang, *Taxation and Governmental Finance in Sixteenth-century* Ming *China*, pp.84-98.
22 *Xin'an xianzhi*, pp.277-78.
23 Ibid., pp.273-75. Also *T.23*.
24 See *T.2*.
25 *Xin'an xianzhi*, pp.280-81.
26 See *T.22*.
27 Wang, *Land Taxation in Imperial China, 1750-1911*, p.32 *et seq.*
28 *Xin'an xianzhi*, p.285.
29 Ibid., pp.285-89.
30 Ibid., p.353.
31 Ibid., pp.353-55.
32 Ho, op.cit., p.101.
33 Wang, op.cit., p.29.
34 Kamm, 'Two Essays on the Ch'ing Economy of Hsin-an, Kwangtung', p.57.
35 Ibid., pp.68-80.
36 Wang, op.cit., p.46.
37 Krone, op.cit., p.124.
38 See especially Potter, *Capitalism and the Chinese Peasant: Social and Economic Change in a Hong Kong Village*; Baker, 'The Five Great Clans of the New Territories' and *A Chinese Lineage Village*; Watson, *Emigration and the Chinese Lineage*; Freedman, 'A Report on Social Research in the New Territories of Hong Kong, 1963', pp.191-261, and *Chinese Lineage and Society: Fukien and Kwangtung*. The Gazetteer makes little reference to lineages, but see *T.13*.
39 Potter, op.cit., p.96; Baker, *A Chinese Lineage Village*, p.171.
40 Baker, *A Chinese Lineage Village*, pp.113-15.
41 Hayes, 'The Pattern of Life in the New Territories in 1898', p.96.
42 See *T.5*.
43 See *T.23*.
44 Krone, op.cit., p.124.
45 *Xin'an xianzhi*, pp.132-37.
46 See *T.47*.
47 Qu, *Guangdong xinyu*, p.486.
48 See *T.47*.
49 *Xin'an xianzhi*, p.295.
50 Hsiao, op.cit., pp.36-39.

51 Huang, op.cit., p.244.
52 *Xin'an xianzhi*, p.295.
53 Ibid., pp.290-95.
54 Huang, op.cit., p.190.
55 Krone, op.cit., p.119.
56 Lin, 'Salt Manufacture in Hong Kong', p.151.
57 *Xin'an xianzhi*, pp.292-93.
58 Ibid., pp.294-95.
59 Krone, op.cit., p.119.
60 *Xin'an xianzhi*, p.294.
61 See *T.48*.
62 See *T.33*.
63 See Baker, *Ancestral Images*, pp.29-32.
64 Groves, 'Militia, Market and Lineage: Chinese Resistance to the Occupation of Hong Kong's New Territories in 1899', p.39. For the workings of the periodic marketing system see Skinner, 'Marketing and Social Structure in Rural China', and Hayes, *The Hong Kong Region 1850-1911*, pp.36-38.
65 *Xin'an xianzhi*, pp.258-61.

4. GOVERNMENT

1 See *T.39*.
2 See *Cihai*, vol. 2, p.2309.
3 Ho, *Studies on the Population of China*, pp.22-23.
4 See *T.22*.
5 Ho, op.cit., p.33.
6 See *T.22*.
7 Lockhart, 'Report by Mr. Stewart Lockhart on the Extension of the Colony of Hong Kong', p.55.
8 See *T.17*.
9 See *T.39*.
10 *Xin'an xianzhi*, p.386.
11 Watt, *The District Magistrate in Late Imperial China*, p.20.
12 See *T.4*.
13 Watt, op.cit., p.14.
14 Quoted in Hayes, 'The Pattern of Life in the New Territories in 1898', p.87.
15 Krone, 'A Notice of the Sanon District', p.125.
16 *Xin'an xianzhi*, p.350.
17 Ibid., pp.246-47.
18 Ibid., p.248.

19 Watt, op.cit., p.12.

20 Hsiao, *Rural China*, p.5.

21 See Ch'ü, *Local Government in China under the Ch'ing*, pp.56-73 for full details.

22 *Guangdong tongzhi, juan* 160.

23 See Ch'ü, op.cit., p.64.

24 See *T.37*.

25 See Fairbank and Teng, *Ch'ing Administration: Three Studies*, pp.1-35.

26 See *T.33*. However, hardly any of the place names on the routes appear on maps, so that the exact routes are impossible to trace.

27 *Guangzhou fuzhi, juan* 2, p.273.

28 Fairbank and Teng, op.cit., pp.13-17.

29 Ch'ü, op.cit., p.132.

30 Krone, op.cit., p.119.

31 Wang, *Land Taxation in Imperial China, 1750-1911*, p.42.

32 Krone, op.cit., p.118.

33 *Xin'an xianzhi*, pp.284-85.

34 See Ch'ü, op.cit., pp.139-40.

35 Ibid., pp.116-29.

36 See *T.39*.

37 See *T.27*, *T.39* and for details see Hsiao, op.cit., pp.184-205.

38 The Sacred Edict was issued in 1670. For translation see Baker, *Chinese Family and Kinship*, p.218.

39 Huc, *The Chinese Empire*, p.228.

40 Krone, op.cit., p.121.

41. See *T.24* and for more details, Hsiao, op.cit., pp.205-220.

42 See *T.41* and *T.42(b)* and *(c)*.

43 *Xin'an xianzhi*, p.179.

44 See for example *T.39*. Also *T.20* and Ch'ü, op.cit., pp.9-10 and pp.161-62.

45 Hsiao, op.cit., p.240. His chapter 'Ideological Control' (pp.184-258) contains a great deal of information on the academy/school system.

46 See Chang, *The Chinese Gentry*, pp.74-75.

47 *Guangdong tongzhi, juan* 172, p.3113.

48 For details of the system see Chang, op.cit., pp.17-18 and pp.134-36.

49 See *T.25*.

50 Chang, op.cit., p.17.

51 *Guangdong tongzhi, juan* 171, pp.3094-95.

52 Ho, *The Ladder of Success in Imperial China*, pp.174-78.

53 See *T.50*.

54 *Guangdong tongzhi, juan* 172, pp.3115-30.

55 See for example Baker, 'The Five Great Clans of the New Territories', pp.32-33; Baker, *A Chinese Lineage Village*, pp.72-73; and Watson, *Emigration and the Chinese Lineage: the Mans in Hong Kong and London*, p.22.

56 See *T.43*.

57 *Xin'an xianzhi*, p.607. For more details of the Liying School see Lo, *Hong Kong and its External Communications before 1842*, pp.133-36.

58 Grimm, 'Academies and Urban Systems in Kwangtung', p.477.

59 See *T.20*.

60 See *T.39*, *T.50* and *Xin'an xianzhi*, p.313.

61 *Xin'an xianzhi*, p.311.

62 See *T.26* and *T.50*.

63 A native of Shangshui in the present New Territories who purchased a Senior Licentiate degree in the early eighteenth century.

64 *Xian'an xianzhi*, pp.312-13.

65 Grimm, op.cit., pp.477-78.

66 Wang, *Hua Xian zhi*, *juan* 3.

67 *Guangzhou fuzhi*, *juan* 34 and *juan* 41.

68 Translated in full at *T.31 and T.32*.

69 Krone, op.cit., p.120.

70 See Ch'ü, op.cit., pp.182-83.

71 See *T.37*.

72 Werner, *A Dictionary of Chinese Mythology*, p.49.

73 See *T.29*.

74 See Baker, *More Ancestral Images*, pp.113-16.

75 See Baker, *Ancestral Images*, pp.1-4 and *T.21*.

76 *Xin'an xianzhi*, p.318.

77 See *T.28*.

78 See for example *T.36* under 1630 and 1673; and *T.37* under 1533 and 1635.

79 Ch'ü, op.cit., p.16.

80 See Mayers, *The Chinese Government*, pp.64-67.

81 See *T.30*.

82 *Xin'an xianzhi*, p.240.

83 For examples see *T.37*.

84 See *Xin'an xianzhi*, pp.349-52 and *T.34*. Mayers, op.cit., pp.64-65 gives a general picture of the military system.

85 See *T.33*.

86 See *T.19*.

87 See *T.30*. The hay was probably for cooking with rather than for fodder, otherwise there would have been no point in a hay ration for Dapeng which had no war horses.

88 *Guangdong tongzhi, juan* 159, pp.2915-16.

89 See for example *Xin'an xianzhi*, p.226.

90 Krone, op.cit., pp.117-18.

91 Davis, *The Chinese: a General Description of the Empire of China and its Inhabitants*, vol. 1, pp.213-14.

92 See *T.34*.

93 See *T.39*.

94 See *T.35*.

95 See *T.37*.

96 Krone, op.cit., p.118.

97 See *T.7*.

98 See *T.47*.

99 See Hsiao, op.cit., pp.43-83.

100 See *T.39*, *T.47* and *T.49*.

101 See Lockhart, op.cit.; Freedman, *Chinese Lineage and Society*; Baker, *A Chinese Lineage Village*; Groves, 'Militia, Market and Lineage: Chinese Resistance to the Occupation of Hong Kong's New Territories in 1899'; Watson, op.cit.; Hayes, *The Hong Kong Region 1850-1911*.

TRANSLATED PASSAGES

1 Some consist of more than one chapter. 'Administration', for instance, is divided into four chapters (8, 9, 10, 11).

2 Scholars, farmers, artisans, merchants.

3 See Ch'ü, *Law and Society in Traditional China*, p.131.

4 The non-Chinese peoples of China were commonly referred to both in writing and speech as *fan* 番 'barbarians', and Westerners were put in the same category.

5 He had been appointed to the post only that year. See *Guangdong tongzhi, juan* 60.

6 One *li* 里 was approximately ⅓ mile.

7 i.e. to Guangzhou and to Beijing respectively.

8 It is probable that 'agriculture' is all that is meant here, the silk-making being more an indicator of 'rural pursuits' than an accurate description.

9 The text here is defective. The translation is based on the text in Hu, *Zhonghua quanguo fengsuzhi, juan* 8, pp.27-28.

10 賤民 : the 'mean people' were socially deprived groups who were not allowed to take the civil service examinations. They included slaves, prostitutes, actors, government runners, beggars, boat-dwellers and their sons. See Ch'ü, op.cit., pp.130-32.

11 The ninth day of the ninth lunar month.

12 A festival fixed by the solar calendar, usually falling on 5 April.
13 A sixth century AD work on customs.
14 These directions should actually be reversed.
15 See Siu, 'The Fat Tong Mun Fort (or the Tung Lung Fort)', pp.209-211.
16 For the functions of these clerks see Ch'ü, *Local Government in China under the Ch'ing*, ch.3.
17 The title of this office is wrongly given as *Dianli* 典吏 instead of *Dianshi* 典史 in the texts.
18 10 *chi* 尺 = 1 *zhang* 丈 = 11.5 feet approximately.
19 Appointed as the first County Magistrate in 1573.
20 This is the terminology of geomancy 風水 , a pseudo-science which talks in terms of benefits to be reaped from harmonizing man's creations with nature.
21 But according to Chapter Five Shi had been promoted elsewhere as a county magistrate in 1594. See *Xin'an xianzhi*, p.176.
22 Took office in 1600.
23 According to *Xin'an xianzhi*, p.178 he actually took office in 1681.
24 Guandi 關帝 was the God of War, but he was also worshipped as a God of Literature.
25 This description tallies quite closely with the general features described by Watters for such buildings, and the various gods in the temple are also in accord with his schema. See Watters, *A Guide to the Tablets in a Temple of Confucius*, pp.v-vii.
26 N.B. These figures do not add up.
27 i.e. Shunzhi period, but exact year omitted in texts.
28 An indication that these population figures were 'taxable values' rather than 'people'. See Ho, *Studies on the Population of China*, p.35.
29 This is the year that the quinquennial *ding* 丁 assessment was abolished. See Ho, op.cit., p.47.
30 Part of the school-temple complex. See *T.20*.
31 Lo Hsiang-lin points out the inadequacy of this quota where the Hakka constituted two-fifths of the population of Xin'an. See Lo, *Yibasiernian yiqian zhi Xianggang jiqi duiwai jiaotong*, pp.214-15, footnote 32.
32 The name of Xu Sun's immediate predecessor Tian Wentao is omitted from the list. His rule can at best have been only short as Xu's appointment was made later the same year (1805).
33 Kuixing 魁星 was a God of Literature.
34 See *T.50*.
35 For more detail of these procedures see Ch'ü, *Local Government in China under the Ch'ing*, pp.164-65.
36 AD 1368-98.

37 Official charitable burial grounds. The idea dated from Song dynasty times.
38 A quotation from the *Li ji*.
39 *Run* 閏 years had thirteen instead of twelve months and occurred seven times in every nineteen years.
40 See Fairbank and Teng, *Ch'ing Administration: Three Studies*, pp.1-35.
41 AD 1506-1521.
42 For more detail on warships and sea-fighting see Qu, *Guangdong xinyu*, *juan* 18, pp.478-80.
43 Probably a black cloud of unusual shape. See under 1630 below.
44 Southern Chinese tend to muddle up snow and ice.
45 Probably the Mexican Dollar.
46 A name applied at this time usually to the Portuguese or Spanish. See Braga, *China Landfall, 1513*, p.63.
47 Lin had a five year term of office as County Magistrate from 1528-33.
48 N.B. this is the same man mentioned in the 1566 incident, though his title is different.
49 The cyclical date given in the text is incorrect, but 1569 seems to be the most likely interpretation.
50 Some details of the battle can be found in the commemorative inscription on that temple reproduced in *Xin'an xianzhi*, ch.23.
51 See Chang, *The Chinese Gentry*, pp.184-86.
52 Lo Hsiang-lin identifies this as Meiwo on Lantau Island, Hong Kong. See Lo, *Hong Kong and its External Communications before 1842*, p.65.
53 See Jen, 'The Travelling Palace of Southern Sung', pp.21-38.
54 AD 420-78.
55 Han Yu 韓愈 (AD 768-824) was a Tang dynasty statesman, poet and philosopher who passed through Guangzhou on his way to take up office at Chaozhou. But he is known to have been opposed to the influence of the Buddhist religion, and this makes it less likely that he would have written the phrase. Lo Hsiang-lin suggests that it is a forgery and was actually written by the Song dynasty scholar Deng Fuxie who was the founder of the great New Territories Deng clan. See Lo, *Hong Kong and its External Communications before 1842*, p.22 and also *T.43(c)*.
56 The cyclical date given in the text cannot be correct.
57 Held office from 1586 to 1589.
58 AD 1102-1106.
59 AD 1107-1187. He actually reigned from 1127 to 1162 when he abdicated.
60 See Sung, 'Legends and Stories of the New Territories: Kam T'in'. See also Baker, 'The Five Great Clans of the New Territories'.
61 Presumably Wang Tingjin, though he did not take office until 1803.
62 Xu was County Magistrate from 1805-1808.

BIBLIOGRAPHY

Baker, H.D.R., 'The Five Great Clans of the New Territories', *Journal of the Hong Kong Branch of the Royal Asiatic Society*, vol. 6 (1966), pp.25-48.

________, *A Chinese Lineage Village: Sheung Shui* (London, 1968).

________, *Ancestral Images* (Hong Kong, 1979).

________, *Chinese Family and Kinship* (London, 1979).

________, *More Ancestral Images* (Hong Kong, 1980).

________, *Ancestral Images Again* (Hong Kong, 1981).

Balfour, S.F., 'Hong Kong before the British', *T'ien Hsia Monthly* (Shanghai), vol. 11-12 (1940-41). Reprinted in *Journal of the Hong Kong Branch of the Royal Asiatic Society*, vol. 10 (1970), pp.134-79.

Bao'an Jintian Dengshi zupu 寶安錦田鄧氏族譜 [Genealogy of the Deng Surname of JinTian in Bao'an]. MS, no date.

Barnett, K.M.A., 'Introduction', in T.R. Tregear, *Hong Kong Gazetteer* (Hong Kong, 1958), pp.1-13.

________, 'Hong Kong before the Chinese', *Journal of the Hong Kong Branch of the Royal Asiatic Society*, vol. 4 (1964), pp.42-67.

________, 'Do Words from Extinct Pre-Chinese Languages Survive in Hong Kong Place-names?', *Journal of the Hong Kong Branch of the Royal Asiatic Society*, vol. 14 (1974), pp.136-59. This is a slightly amended version of his 1958 'Introduction'.

Beijing Review (Beijing), no. 6 (9 February 1979).

Braga, J.M., *China Landfall, 1513* (Hong Kong, 1956).

Burkhardt, V.R., *Chinese Creeds and Customs*. 3 vols. (Hong Kong, 1953, 1955, 1958).

Chang Chung-li, *The Chinese Gentry* (Washington, 1955).

Chang, K.C. (ed.), *Food in Chinese Culture: Anthropological and Historical Perspectives* (New Haven, 1977).

Char, T.K. and Kwock, C.H., *The Hakka Chinese — their Origin and Folk Songs* (San Francisco, 1969).

Chongxiu Xin'an xianzhi 重修新安縣志 [Revised Xin'an County Gazetteer], compiled by Jin Wenmo 靳文謨 , Deng Wenwei 鄧文蔚 *et al*. (1688 康熙戊辰).

Ch'ü T'ung-tsu, *Local Government in China under the Ch'ing* (Harvard, 1962).

________, *Law and Society in Traditional China* (Paris, 1965).

Cihai 辭海 . 3 vols. (Shanghai, 1979).

Davis, J.F., *The Chinese: a General Description of the Empire of China and its Inhabitants.* 2 vols. (London, 1836).

De Groot, J.J.M., *The Religious System of China.* 6 vols. (Leyden, 1892-1910).

District Commissioner, New Territories, *Annual Departmental Report*, 1970-71 (Hong Kong, 1971).

Endacott, G.B., *A History of Hong Kong* (London, 1958).

Fairbank, J.K. and Teng, S.Y., *Ch'ing Administration: Three Studies* (Harvard, 1960).

Finn, Daniel J., S.J., *Archaeological Finds on Lamma Island near Hong Kong* (Hong Kong, 1958).

Freedman, Maurice, 'A Report on Social Research in the New Territories of Hong Kong 1963' (mimeo; 1963). Reprinted in *Journal of the Hong Kong Branch of the Royal Asiatic Society*, vol. 16 (1976) pp.191-261.

________, *Chinese Lineage and Society: Fukien and Kwangtung* (London, 1966).

A Gazetteer of Place Names in Hong Kong, Kowloon and the New Territories (Hong Kong, 1960).

Grant, C.J., *The Soils and Agriculture of Hong Kong* (Hong Kong, 1960.)

Grimm, Tilemann, 'Academies and Urban Systems in Kwangtung' in G.W. Skinner (ed.), *The City in Late Imperial China* (Stanford, 1977), pp.475-98.

Groves, R.G., 'Militia, Market and Lineage: Chinese Resistance to the Occupation of Hong Kong's New Territories in 1899', *Journal of the Hong Kong Branch of the Royal Asiatic Society*, vol. 9 (1969), pp.31-64.

Guangdong tongzhi 廣東通志 [A Gazetteer of Guangdong], edited by Ruan Yuan 阮元 . Page references are to the Taiwan Shudian 臺灣書店 edition. 4 vols. (Taipei, 1959).

Guangdong wenwu 廣東文物 [Cultural Relics of Guangdong]. 4 vols. (Guangzhou, 1941).

Guangzhou fuzhi 廣州府志 [A Gazetteer of Guangzhou], compiled by Rui Lin 瑞麟 and Dai Zhaochen 戴肇辰 . Page numbers refer to the Chengwen Chubanshe 成文出版社 edition. 3 vols. (Taipei, 1966).

Han Yu 韓愈 (AD 768-824), 'Zengbie Yuan Shiba xielü' 贈別元十八協律 [A Farewell Poem to Yuan], in *Han Changli ji* 韓昌黎集 [Collected Works of Han Yu], *juan* 6.

Hashimoto, Mantaro J., *The Hakka Dialect: a Linguistic Study of its Phonology, Syntax and Lexicon* (Cambridge, 1973).

Hayes, James, 'The Pattern of Life in the New Territories in 1898', *Journal of the Hong Kong Branch of the Royal Asiatic Society*, vol. 2 (1962), pp.75-102.

________, 'The San On Map of Mgr. Volontieri [sic]', *Journal of the Hong Kong*

Branch of the Royal Asiatic Society, vol. 10 (1970), pp.193-96.

________, *The Hong Kong Region 1850-1911* (Hamden, Conn., 1977).

He Guangmo 何光謨, 'Lun fangzhi zai shijizhongde diwei ji gongyong' 論方志在史籍中的地位及功用 [The Place and Function of the Gazetteer in Historical Records]. Foreword to *Guangdong tushuo* 廣東圖說 [An Illustrative Description of Guangdong] (Taipei, 1967).

Ho Kê-ên 何格恩, 'A Study of the Boat People (with 5 maps)' 蜑族之研究, *Journal of Oriental Studies* (Hong Kong), vol. 5 (1959-60), pp.1-39.

Ho Ping-ti, *Studies on the Population of China, 1368-1953* (Harvard, 1959).

________, *The Ladder of Success in Imperial China* (New York, 1962).

Hong Kong 1981 (Hong Kong, Hong Kong Government Information Services, 1981).

Hsiao Kung-chuan, *Rural China: Imperial Control in the Nineteenth Century* (Seattle, 1960).

Hsieh Kuo Ching, 'Removal of Coastal Population in Early Tsing Period', *The Chinese Social and Political Science Review*, vol. 15 (1931-32), pp.559-96.

Hu Puan 胡樸安, *Zhonghua quanguo fengsuzhi* 中華全國風俗志, [A Record of the Customs of the Chinese Nation] (Taipei, 1968).

Huang, Ray, *Taxation and Governmental Finance in Sixteenth-century Ming China* (London, 1974).

Huc, M., *The Chinese Empire* (London, 1859).

Hucker, Charles O., 'Governmental Organization of the Ming Dynasty', in J.L. Bishop (ed.), *Studies of Governmental Institutions in Chinese History* (Harvard, 1968).

Hummel, A.W. (ed.), *Eminent Chinese of the Ch'ing Period* (Washington, 1943-44).

Ingrams, Harold, *Hong Kong* (London, 1952).

The Journal of the Hong Kong Archaeological Society (Hong Kong, 1968 —).

Journal of the Hong Kong Branch of the Royal Asiatic Society (Hong Kong, 1961 —).

Jen, Yu-wen, 'The Travelling Palace of Southern Sung', *Journal of the Hong Kong Branch of the Royal Asiatic Society*, vol. 7 (1967), pp.21-38.

Kamm, J.T., 'Two Essays on the Ch'ing Economy of Hsin-an, Kwangtung', *Journal of the Hong Kong Branch of the Royal Asiatic Society*, vol. 17 (1977), pp.55-84.

Kani, Hiroaki, *A General Survey of the Boat People in Hong Kong* (Hong Kong, 1967).

Krone, Rev. Mr., 'A Notice of the San On District', *Transactions of the China Branch of the Royal Asiatic Society* (Hong Kong, 1859), pp.71-105. Reprinted in *Journal of the Hong Kong Branch of the Royal Asiatic Society*, vol. 7 (1967) pp.104-137.

Li ji 禮記 [The Book of Rites].

Lim Tien-wai 林天蔚, 'Nan-Song shi Dayu Shan wei Yaoqu zhi shizheng' 南宋時大嶼山爲傜區之試證 [Was Lantau Island a Yao Area in the Southern Song], *The Chung Chi Journal* (Hong Kong) 崇基學報, vol. 3, no. 2 (May 1964), pp.175-89.

Lin, S.Y., 'Salt Manufacture in Hong Kong', *The Hong Kong Naturalist*, vol. X, no. 1 (1940). Reprinted in *Journal of the Hong Kong Branch of the Royal Asiatic Society*, vol. 7 (1967), pp.138-51.

Lo Hsiang-lin 羅香林, *Kejia yanjiu taolun* 客家硏究討論 [Researches on the Hakka] (Taipei, 1933). Japanese translation 1942.

________ 'The Sung Wang T'ai and the Location of the Travelling Courts by the Sea-shore in the Last Days of the Sung', *Journal of Oriental Studies*, vol. 3 (1956), pp.185-217.

________ (ed.), *Yibasiernian yiqian zhi Xianggang jiqi duiwai jiaotong* 一八四二年以前之香港及其對外交通 [Hong Kong and its External Communications before 1842] (Hong Kong, 1959).

________ (ed.), *Hong Kong and its External Communications before 1842* (Hong Kong, 1963). This is an English language edition of the preceding, but without the full notes of the Chinese version.

Lo Wan, 'Communal Strife in Mid-nineteenth-century Kwangtung', *Papers on China* (Harvard), vol. 19 (1965), pp.85-119.

Lockhart, J.H.S., 'Report by Mr. Stewart Lockhart on the Extension of the Colony of Hong Kong', *Eastern*, No.66 (8 October 1898) (Colonial Office, 1900).

Mayers, W.F., *The Chinese Government* (Shanghai, 1897).

McCoy, John, 'The Dialects of Hong Kong Boat People: Kau Sai', *Journal of the Hong Kong Branch of the Royal Asiatic Society*, vol. 5 (1965), pp.46-64.

Meacham, William, *Archaeology in Hong Kong* (Hong Kong, 1980).

Needham, Joseph, *Science and Civilization in China*, vol. 3 (Cambridge, 1959).

Ng, Ronald C.Y., 'The San On map of Mgr. Volonteri', *Journal of the Hong Kong Branch of the Royal Asiatic Society*, vol. 9 (1969), pp.141-48. Originally published in the same year in the *Geographical Journal*, vol. 135, pp.231-35.

Nivison, David S., *The Life and Thought of Chang Hsüeh-ch'eng (1738-1801)* (Stanford, 1966).

Peplow, S.H. and Barker, M., *Hongkong, Around and About* (Hong Kong, 1931).

Potter, Jack M., *Capitalism and the Chinese Peasant: Social and Economic Change in a Hong Kong Village* (Berkeley, 1968).

Qu Dajun 屈大均, *Guangdong xinyu* 廣東新語 [New Tales of Guangdong] (1700). Page references are given to the Zhonghua Shuju 中華書局 edition (Hong Kong, 1974).

Schafer, Edward, *The Vermilion Bird: T'ang Images of the South* (Berkeley, 1967).

Siak, P.L., 'Traditional Farming Techniques and their Survival in Hong Kong', *Journal of the Hong Kong Branch of the Royal Asiatic Society*, vol. 14 (1974), pp.191-96.

Siu Kwok-kin, 'The Fat Tong Mun Fort (or the Tung Lung Fort)', *Journal of the Hong Kong Branch of the Royal Asiatic Society*, vol. 18 (1978), pp.209-211.

Skinner, G.W., 'Marketing and Social Structure in Rural China', *Journal of Asian Studies*, vol. XXIV, nos. 1-3 (1964-65).

Sung Hok-p'ang, 'Legends and Stories of the New Territories: Kam T'in', *The Hong Kong Naturalist* (1935-8). Reprinted in *Journal of the Hong Kong Branch of the Royal Asiatic Society*, vol. 13 (1973), pp.111-29 and vol. 14 (1974), pp.160-85.

Volonteri, Mgr. Simeone, *Map of the San-On-District (Kwangtung Province). Drawn from Actual Observations made by an Italian Missionary of the Propaganda* (Leipzig, 1866).

Wang, Yeh-chien, *Land Taxation in Imperial China, 1750-1911* (Cambridge, Mass., 1973).

Wang Yong-ming 王永名, *(Hua Xian zhi* 花縣志 [A Gazetteer of Hua Xian] (1890 光緒庚寅).

Ward, Barbara E., 'A Hong Kong Fishing Village', *Journal of Oriental Studies* (Hong Kong), vol. 1, no. 1 (1954), pp.195-214.

Watson, James L., *Emigration and the Chinese Lineage: the Mans in Hong Kong and London* (Berkeley, 1975).

Watt, John R., *The District Magistrate in Late Imperial China* (New York, 1972).

Watters, T., *A Guide to the Tablets in a Temple of Confucius* (Shanghai, 1879).

Werner, E.T.C., *A Dictionary of Chinese Mythology* (Shanghai, 1932).

Wiens, Herold J., *Han Chinese Expansion in South China* (Hamden, Conn, 1967).

Wong, F.L. 黃福鑾, 'Zhongyuan minzuzhi nanqian yu Guangdong wenhua zhi fazhan' 中原民族之南遷與廣東文化之發展 [The Migration of the Han Nation and the Development of Guangdong Culture], *The Chung Chi Journal* (Hong Kong 崇基學報, vol. 1, no. 1 (July 1961), pp.4-15.

Xin'an xianzhi 新安縣志 [Xin'an Gazetteer], compiled by Wang Chongxi 王崇熙, Shu Maoguan 舒懋官 *et al.* (1819 嘉慶己卯). Page references are to the Chengwen Chubanshe 成文出版社 edition. 2 vols. (Taipei, 1974).

Xiang Da 向達, *Man Shu jiaozhu* 蠻書校註 [A Commentary on the Man Shu] (Beijing, 1962).

Xin Tang shu 新唐書 [A New History of the Tang Dynasty]. 20 vol. (Beijing, 1975).

Xue Zhongsan and Ouyang Yi, *A Sino-Western Calendar for Two Thousand Years, 1-2000 AD* (Hong Kong, 1961).

INDEX

WEIGHTS AND MEASURES

(Approximate equivalents only)

LENGTH

li 里 = 0.31 miles
zhang 丈 = 3.65 yards
chi 尺 = 1.1 feet

GRAIN MEASURES

dan 石 = 2.75 bushels
dou 斗 = 2.2 gallons
sheng 升 = 0.28 pints

WEIGHT

catty 斤 = 1.33 lb. av.
tael 兩 = 1.33 oz. av. (used as a unit of silver currency)

AREA

qing 頃 = 16.5 acres
mu 畝 = 0.165 acre
The *mu* was further subdivided decimally into *fen* 分 , then *li* 厘 , then *hao* 毫 , then *si* 絲 , and finally into *hu* 忽 (= 1/100,000 *mu*).